Additional praise for *Cyber Threat! How to Manage the Growing Risk of Cyber Attacks*

"Don Ulsch has written a provocative and informative book that is a must-read for all board members. You cannot protect against risks you are not aware of, and, although at times his message is scary, Don certainly lays out the cyber risks companies face."

—**Debra Squires-Lee**, Partner, Sherin and Lodgen, LLP

"Don Ulsch's new book is a passionate, sincere, and thorough analysis of the problem of cyber attacks, in all of its aspects. The Introduction title, "What Every Current and Future Senior Executive Must Know about the Cyber Threat," summarizes perfectly the vast content of Don's book. One does not have to be a senior executive in order to understand, appreciate, and enjoy Don's book. A must-read, definitely."

—**Dimitris Zografopoulos, PhD,** Legal Auditor at
Hellenic Data Protection Authority, Member of DAPIX
Working Group on Information Exchange and
Data Protection–Council of European Union

"Don Ulsch provides a great summary of the threats that companies face in cyberspace. It is only with awareness of the real threats that organizations face that executives can take the appropriate actions to protect their companies."

—**Ira Winkler,** President, Secure Mentem

"As a CISO and enterprise risk professional, I found the topics covered insightful and well-timed. Cyber threat spreads fire to the risk landscape and gives a realistic, useful, and fact-based education for the senior-level executive."

—**Nikk Gilbert, CISSP, CISM,** Vice President and
Chief Information Security Officer,

"The time to hide from the cyber threat is over, thanks to this book: a useful tool to protect your corporation, your family, and yourself from a cyber attack. Another example of Don's wisdom."

—**Manuel González Alonso,** former Spanish Police Chief Inspector, Security Chief,
Criminologist, Detective, and current
Chief Executive Officer in "DARTE Investigación Privada"

"The loss of security around our most valued information has become an enormous drain on our national resources and is disruptive to our everyday lives. The source of risks is not always what they appear to be. Mr. Ulsch's sage advice and counsel helps each of us who handle or manage important information limit our exposure and loss of information."

—**Danny Miller,** System Chief Information Security Officer,
Office of the Chief Information Officer,
the Texas A&M University System

"Don has dedicated his professional career to researching and educating various industry groups about cyber security, and he is truly a global expert. Don clearly explains cyber security threats originating from sources domestic and foreign, how cyber attacks are perpetrated, and why organized crime, terrorist organizations, and some countries are winning the cyber war. *Cyber Threat!* alerts readers as to how and why electronic information is at risk and provides solutions on how to protect this information."

—**Thomas Alger,** Director of Risk Management, Mass Development

"Don has given the information security community a very insightful book, which will assist us in navigating an increasingly turbulent, pervasive, ever-evolving cybersecurity landscape, by providing an abundance of essential knowledge. *Cyber Threat!* answers the pertinent questions that all CISOs should be asking in the year 2014. If you are looking for some of the missing pieces to the global information security puzzle or simply want to understand the current cybersecurity reality to which we must awaken each morning, then *Cyber Threat* is a must-read."

—**Bob Ganim,** Chief Information Security Officer, Global Investment Management Firm

"This easy-to-read, yet highly informative, book exposes the frightening truth about the growing risk of the increasingly sophisticated cyber attacks that threaten businesses today. Written in a snappy, nontechnical style, the author explains key facts and policy considerations using engaging stories and illustrative anecdotes. Throughout the book, the reader is presented with sensible recommendations and enterprise governance strategies to deal with these threats. This is an essential read for corporate executives and members of boards of directors."

—**David R. Wilson, Esq.,** President, Gateway Associates

"*Cyber Threat!* clearly sets the scene for today's challenges in this arena. Don addresses the global threat environment head-on and then discusses essential ways to protect intellectual property, infrastructure, and corporate reputation. It is a must-read for all IT security and compliancy professionals."

—**David A. Wilkinson,** The Bellwether Group, Inc.

"The corporate board room is under attack from many sides, the most concerning of which is the threat of cyber crimes. Don Ulsch is uniquely qualified to provide effective protection techniques to ensure that the integrity of corporate information is maintained at the highest level. This book is a must-read for all levels of management in both the private and public sector."

—**Donald P. Hart, Esq.,** Nantucket, Massachusetts

"We've embarked on the 'Internet of things' without a clear understanding of what it will mean to our digital and personal lives. Don gives us the undeniable facts that every board member and corporate executive should read. You can't ignore the truth after you read this book."

—**Patricia Titus,** Vice President and Chief Information Security Officer, Freddie Mac

Cyber Threat!

The Wiley Corporate F&A series provides information, tools, and insights to corporate professionals responsible for issues affecting the profitability of their company, from accounting and finance to internal controls and performance management.

Founded in 1807, John Wiley & Sons is the oldest independent publishing company in the United States. With offices in North America, Europe, Asia, and Australia, Wiley is globally committed to developing and marketing print and electronic products and services for our customers' professional and personal knowledge and understanding.

Cyber Threat!

How to Manage the Growing Risk of Cyber Attacks

N. MacDONNELL ULSCH

WILEY

Cover image: © iStock.com / michelangelus
Cover design: Wiley

Library of Congress Cataloging-in-Publication Data:
Ulsch, N. MacDonnell, 1951–
Cyber threat! : how to manage the growing risk of cyber attacks / N. MacDonnell Ulsch.
    pages cm – (Wiley corporate F&A Series)
Includes index.
  ISBN 978-1-118-83635-4 (hardback); ISBN 978-1-118-93595-8 (epub);
ISBN 978-1-118-935969-5 (epdf); ISBN 978-1-118-91502-8 (obook)
  1. Corporations—Security measures. 2. Business enterprises—Computer networks—Security measures. 3. Computer crimes—Prevention. 4. Computer security. 5. Computer networks—Security measures. I. Title.
  HD30.2.U47 2014
  658.4'78—dc23
                                                                    2014012281

Printed in the United States of America

10 9 8 7 6 5 4 3 2 1

To my wife, Susan Shea Ulsch, my mother, Evelyn Frankenberg Houck, my brother, Phillip Ulsch, and his wife, Josie, my daughter, Jeanne McCabe, and Kenneth Brown. Around them, and their own growing families, my own universe revolves. To Joseph and Margaret Frankenberg, and N. M. Ulsch Sr. And to those in our family who fought overseas for the enduring liberty we enjoy years after their sacrifice: N. M. Ulsch Jr., Edward Frankenberg, Joseph Frankenberg, and Archie Shea.

Contents

Foreword

Like a red morn that even betokened, Wreck to
the seaman, tempest to the field, Sorrow to the
shepherds, woe unto the birds, Gusts and foul
flaws to herdsmen and to herds.

—*Shakespeare, Venus and Adonis (1593)*

F IT has been some time since you have read and studied Shakespeare,
let me offer another version of the warning in the epigraph:

Red sky in the morning—Sailors take warning.

—*Author, unknown*

Don Ulsch has once again, in his most recent book, clearly explained the
cyber threat risks. This threat became crystal clear to me, when, as U.S.
Attorney for the District of Massachusetts, I was approached by a U.S.-based
Fortune 150 company that was being extorted by an organized crime syndicate, operating with impunity, in an eastern European country. The demand:
cash. The risk for the company: the loss of years of product research and
development and hundreds of millions of dollars of future revenue.

Frustratingly, the organized crime syndicate operated in a place beyond
the reach of our federal government resources. The lessons I learned during
that investigation were the great and growing cyber risks faced by U.S.
companies and the limited abilities of our government to protect those

companies and their shareholders from this harm. It is morning in corporate America, and many are facing a red sky.

Notwithstanding this real and escalating harm that costs our government, consumers, and the private sector billions in losses, far too many executives continue to ignore the "perfect storm" we are facing.

Louis Pasteur once said, "Chance favors the prepared mind." Don Ulsch explains how chance also favors the prepared company.

When Thomas Alva Edison said "Genius is 1% inspiration and 99% perspiration," his idea of perspiration was hard work, not worry. To be successful in protecting a company's assets from today's threats requires 99 percent preparation and 1 percent perspiration. For those executives who view their companies as less than 99 percent prepared, Don Ulsch's book is just the right prescription. And like the early sailor viewing the sunset, the benefits for those prepared executives will be a "red sky at night—and the executives delight."

—Michael Sullivan
Partner
Ashcroft Law Firm
Kansas City, Missouri

Preface

WHERE TO begin? Start with the fundamental assertion that we are at war, a cyber war. The topic is expansive and seems to become more inclusive every day as the word "cyber" enters almost every aspect of our lives. "Cyber" is becoming so familiar to us now that we passively accept anything associated with it. We don't always appreciate that, but it is true, and it becomes truer with every new day and Internet-enabled device. We don't see all of these devices, either. From laptops and smartphones and tablets to automobiles to refrigerators, cockpits, and smart homes, we are connected. The utilities that power our inventions and domiciles are connected. Hospitals are connected. Retail stores, insurance companies, defense contractors, automobile manufacturers are connected, too, as are chemical manufacturers, agriculture, and government. It seems like everyone is connected to everything, and all is connected to or by the Internet.

And that's great—or so it seems. But the bad actors of the world, from organized criminals to narcotics traffickers to identity thieves to traffickers of humans, sex, illegal arms, and even weapons of mass destruction, have also found a cyber stage upon which to perform.

This book is about three defined issues. First is the cyber threat. Growing worse by the day, it is omnipresent, diversified, giving the word "cyber" a bad reputation. Cyber love, cyber kindness, cyber humility, cyber goodness, cyber cheer—these terms are vastly outgunned by other cyber-ish terms. Cyber war, cyber terror, cyber bullying, cyber fraud, cyber spying, cyber crime come to mind.

Second is the notion of vulnerability. What makes us vulnerable, and what increases this vulnerability? Things like social media contribute to this state of vulnerability. So does mobility, a culture of information on demand, anywhere, anytime, and on any device. It seems the more information-rich and information-device diverse we become, the more vulnerable we become. Somewhat insidiously, the more vulnerable we become, the less we may realize it. Why? Because we are so intimately familiar with all things cyber. Cyber haunts the backstory of most everything we do. It is invisible. Only its symbols are seemingly magically visible. Its commonness instills if not a sense of trust, then one of virtual indifference. As with a colorful toy, we are mesmerized with cyber things, even if the word is never uttered. Games, maps, menus, books, movies, lectures, newspapers, magazines, and just about everything else is digital.

The third undertaking is what enterprises can do to help offset the threats by addressing vulnerabilities. Interestingly enough, governments are trying to reduce the threats through public policy, regulation, security guidelines, and frameworks. However, there is no escaping the fact that every organization must face these issues, with or without input and insight from the government. These are not assignable risks. This book examines some of the things organizations, from government to public and private enterprises, should do to prepare for what many consider to be an inevitable breach. No organization is helpless. Far from it. The issue isn't that there's nothing to do, that we're totally defenseless. It's more that the synaptic charges that are supposed to get through to the boards lose thrust and intensity along the way.

Ralph Waldo Emerson once wrote that nothing great ever happens without enthusiasm. One of the great things that can be done in the face of the powerful cyber threat is simply to accept it, confront it head-on, and commit to managing the risks it conveys. There is an opportunity to generate enthusiasm about managing the cyber threat, about mitigating the risks it poses.

Divided into three parts, this book conveys the message that "security" and "technology" are two words that every board director must embrace, because these two words result in two other words that the board understands all too well: "risk impact." Part I examines the cyber threat in its many forms. Part II takes a look at the vulnerabilities common to companies, while Part III provides strategies for more effectively controlling the risks associated with cyber attacks.

This book hopes to instill that enthusiasm by discussing the threat, examining the vulnerabilities, and embracing change that leads to more resilience and resistance to the threat. But one thing is certain: Cyber crime is like any other crime. It isn't going away. Just the opposite seems true. And a cyber war defines war. No war in the future will take place without this dimension. We live in a digital universe, for better or worse. Make no mistake. We need to manage the cyber element of our universe so that it does not manage us. The greatest risk is in failing to meet this threat.

Acknowledgments

WHILE ONE person may be responsible for actually writing a book, it is by no means a solitary pursuit. Certainly that was the case with *Cyber Threat!* My thinking about the evolution of the asymmetric cyber threat has been shaped by many people whose opinions and perspectives I respect. While we do not always agree on every issue, I do believe that the big cyber threat picture is coming clearly into focus and that we agree on many aspects of the problem and the solutions. Unhesitatingly, I would say that without their contributions, this book would not have been possible. In many ways this is a race against time, a race to close the gaps before the digital barbarians get through the gate. On that we all agree. Whatever deficiencies this volume may suffer are the fault of the author, not those who generously contributed their time and expertise.

The cyber threat is not just a computer or technology issue. It is a fundamental business and industry issue, comprised of technology and human behavior. It is a problem that has leached into virtually every dimension and aspect of life. As a threat, it packs a powerful blow. Balancing the threat against the necessity of all things cyber is a delicate exercise. As they say, it's complicated. It also requires many vantage points. I have been fortunate in receiving many perspectives on the subject.

Writing a book is a family affair, and this one was no exception. All we have is time, and how we spend it matters. I felt this was an important subject, and so did my family, and it was therefore worth the commitment. This book would not have been possible without the love and support of my family.

First, a special thanks to my wife, Susan, who is a tireless researcher and constant editor who continuously challenges assumptions and supported this effort from day one. My mother, Evelyn Houck, also encouraged the effort and supported it in many ways. My brother, Phillip, of the Maverick Insurance Agency, provided special insight on cyber insurance and risk. Kenneth Brown, an adviser at ZeroPoint Risk Research where I worked for nearly five years, proved to be a strong sounding board about banking, the economy, and risk management.

Michael J. Sullivan of the Ashcroft Sullivan LLC law firm deserves special thanks, and not only for contributing the foreword of this book. Mike has dedicated much of his career to public service and personifies what it means to serve, most recently as the U.S. attorney for the District of Massachusetts and as director of the Bureau of Alcohol, Tobacco, Firearms and Explosives. He has prosecuted war criminals, terrorists, and cyber criminals, among others. Mike dedicated his invaluable time in discussing the issues examined in this book. Working with Mike are an exemplary group of professionals, including former U.S. assistant attorney Brian J. Leske, attorney Ellen Giblin, attorney Amy Barry, and Michelle Reilly, who are always professional, resourceful, and supportive and who have contributed selflessly. I also want to thank former U.S. attorney general John Ashcroft, David Ayers, and Paul Garrett of the Ashcroft Group LLC.

Ken Mortensen, former associate deputy attorney general, spent many hours with me at the Patriot Diner discussing transnational organized crime, privacy, and many other cyber threat issues. I would also like to express my gratitude to Thomas Garruba for his insights. A number of executives at Boston Private Bank and Trust Company were generous with their time and expertise, including Chief Risk Officer Timothy MacDonald, Rich Byron, attorney Victoria Kane, William Kane, Christine Cioffi, and Tiffany DeMontier.

My sincerest thanks to attorneys Heather Egan Sussman of the Boston office of McDermott, Emery & Will LLP, and attorneys Jennifer Geeter and Jon Dabney of the Washington, D.C., office. All have been a pleasure to work with, often under trying circumstances, and all three are exceptional.

I owe special gratitude to my former ZeroPoint Risk Research partners and colleagues Lorie Skolski, Gerard Kane, Steve Grosso, and former FBI special agent and security executive Joseph DeSalvo. They were always unwavering in their support and are dedicated professionals for whom I have exceptional regard.

To former Boston police commissioner Edward F. Davis, thank you. Catapulted into the national spotlight during the Boston Marathon terrorist bombing in 2013, he was a tireless figure when it seemed Boston was under siege.

Attorneys William "Bill" Rogers, John F. Bradley, and Peter J. Caruso of Prince Lobel Tye LLP in Boston have been generous with their time and expertise, as has former federal prosecutor Joseph M. Burton, managing partner of the San Francisco office of Duane Morris LLP, and Eduard Goodman of ID

Theft 911. Dr. Lothar Determann, an attorney at Baker & McKenzie LLP, has been very helpful, and I appreciate his expertise and efforts. I extend my thanks to Holly Chase, a bank regulator and expert in financial institution risk, and to Elton Hill, who retired recently from the Federal Reserve. I also want to acknowledge Kevin Hamel, who leads the privacy and security initiative at COCC.

For many years I have been associated with the National Security Institute. Thank you to my NSI colleagues Stephen Burns, David Marston, and the late Edward Hymoff. Much of what I know about security I learned at NSI. It was Ed, formerly with the forerunner of the Central Intelligence Agency, the Office of Strategic Services, who one day a number of years ago, while I was teaching at Boston University, said, "There are a couple of former military guys I'd like you to meet." It was Dave and Steve. A great American and national treasure also serves on the advisory board of the National Security Institute, four-star General Earl Anderson, U.S. Marine Corps (Retired), the youngest active-duty Marine ever promoted to the rank of general. He is also the former assistant commandant of the Marine Corps. At this writing he is 94 years old. Semper Fi, General.

For their invaluable contributions over the years I would like to thank attorney David R. Wilson, John Cassella, Thomas Barrett, and Colonel James Bullion, U.S. Army (Retired). Colonel Bullion served two tours in Iraq and has spent a great deal of time in Afghanistan with the Department of Defense, where understanding the nature of threats and responding accordingly is essential to survival.

Retired Marine Corps officers and National Security Agency veterans Ed Lucke and Jeffrey Zimmerman have long been colleagues whose experiences also shaped my appreciation of threat and risk. Dr. Larry Ponemon and Susan Jayson of the Ponemon Institute have been very supportive, encouraging, and generous with their research. I would like to thank Jerry Archer, Jim Malatesta, Jin Kim, Richard Crawford, Phill Bakker, Joe Judge, Jeffrey Bamberger, Dr. Angelo Tosi, and John Rostern for their observations and support over the years. Thank you also to Thomas Wagner for your advice and counsel.

Anthony Kimery, executive editor of *Homeland Security Today*, has been extremely helpful and insightful and always supportive. Thank you, Christopher Pierson, for your studied perspective on privacy, and Tom Alger. Andy Briney of TechTarget is always helpful, and I have appreciated his counsel and observations through the years. I also want to acknowledge Kathleen Richards and Eric Parizo of TechTarget, as well as Eileen Feretic of *Baseline* magazine.

Thank you, Elizabeth C. and T. Brooks Fitzsimmons.

To Brian Powers, David Mechanic, Dennis Huaman, Maryalice Decamp, Brian Kelly, Chris Winn, Christo Ovcharov, Paul Rozek, Beth Healy, David Welch, Captain G. Mark Hardy, U.S. Navy (Retired), attorney Annemarie McAvoy of Fordham University Law School, Gary Foster, and Dr. Jack Kerivan, thank you for your continuous support and encouragement. Michael Fountain and Mike Weir, thank you.

Also deserving of thanks are Thomas E. Samoluk, attorney, executive, and author, whose commentary on certain subjects has proved spine-tingling, Anne Marie Graceffa, and David Rawlings. Dan Swartwood of the Ponemon Institute and president of the Society for the Policing of the Cyberspace, thank you for your insights. Debra Squires-Lee of Sherin Lodgen LLP is deserving of thanks. John Colucci of the McLane law firm, thanks for your frequent counsel. I appreciate the contribution of Nicola Crawford of i-Risk Europe Ltd. Much appreciation to Nikk Gilbert, CISO of CUNA Mutual, and Naheed Bleecker for their continuing support. To Kevin Hamel, vice president of security at COCC, thank you for your observations and support. To Eileen Turcotte, thank you.

I want to extend my appreciation to Neil Doherty and to attorney Scott Kannry for their always interesting observations regarding privacy and risk.

To David Wilkinson and Karen E. Antons of the Bellwether Group Inc., and M. J. Vaidya, an adjunct professor at New York University and Americas CISO at General Motors, your support is appreciated. Thank you, Constantine Karbaliotis, for your expert counsel, and to Catherine A. Allen and Robin Slade of the Santa Fe Group.

Tomas Filipiak served overseas as an officer in the U.S. Army as an information security professional and understands the cyber threat and its life and death implications in a combat zone. I appreciate his observations. To Matthew Lion, Erin Weber, Sanjay Deo of 24by7 Security LLC, and Clay Moegenberg, I appreciate your always interesting perspective and support. Insurance executive and privacy and security specialist John Graham of Zurich North America was very helpful, as always, and my appreciation goes also to Jim Randall, who is head of global cyber security for Zurich. Danny Miller, system CISO of the Texas A&M University System, was very helpful.

Much of the effort to protect consumers in the United States against the cyber threat is undertaken by states. None is more deserving of mention than the Commonwealth of Massachusetts. Leading this effort are Barbara Anthony, undersecretary of the Office of Consumer Affairs and Business Regulation, and her exceptional team, including Deputy General Counsel Joanne Campo, Julian W. Smith, and Maureen Tobin—thanks for your good work and leadership.

My appreciation is also extended to Paul D'Ambrosio, MD, Andrew DiLernia, MD, and Karyn M. Connolly.

Benjamin Dubuc traveled to China to teach English after graduating from the University of New Hampshire and kept in touch on the cyber threat there, which was greatly appreciated.

Stacey Rivera, my editor at John Wiley & Sons, has proved to be more than patient and exceptionally competent, and I want to thank her for making this book better than it otherwise would have been.

Maintaining integrity in the enterprise is the job of everyone, but the actions of those security, compliance, and privacy officers are vital. Thanks to those whose battle every day is to defend against the cyber threat.

Last but not least, there are others who deserve thanks but their identities will have to remain confidential, as they continue to work behind the scenes in the interest of law enforcement and national security. You know who you are, and I appreciate your work, as do many others.

What Every Current and Future Senior Executive Must Know about the Cyber Threat

A Perfect Digital Storm Is Forming

A "PERFECT STORM" has been described as a combination of circumstances that aggravate or intensify a situation. The 1997 book *The Perfect Storm*, by Sebastian Junger, describes the events of a perfect meteorological storm formed in the fall of 1991. The swordfishing boat *Andrea Gail*, sailing out of Gloucester, Massachusetts, was lost 575 miles off the New England coast to one of the worst storms in maritime history. I often think about that storm when considering the cyber threat.

We are, arguably, experiencing a set of circumstances that significantly intensify the impact of the cyber attacks that occur all the time. Let me be clear. I am not forecasting one such perfect storm, resulting in a catastrophic digital Pearl Harbor strike against the United States that disables critical infrastructure, from the distribution of electricity to the movement of money across the financial system. Of course, that could happen. But I am talking about enterprises large and small, commercial and governmental, that operate continuously under a range of perfect storm-like conditions. These cyber attacks have a telling and sometimes material impact on the organization.

But which organizations? In the February 5, 2013, edition of the *Wall Street Journal*, the editorial writers remarked that "On a visit to our offices last year, a U.S. lawmaker with knowledge of intelligence affairs explained that, when it comes to cyber-espionage, there are only two kinds of American companies these days: Those that have been hacked, and those that don't know they've been hacked."[1]

Perhaps not *every* company has been hacked, but that lawmaker's comment is not far off the mark. Given just the number of breaches of personal information, including health data, reported in the press, it is easy to believe that the problem is extremely serious. But then consider all the breaches that never appear in the media. These are breaches of information integrity that are not reported, for a number of reasons. One reason is that when some companies are breached, management is not aware of any obligation to report the breach to U.S. federal or state or even foreign-country regulators. While it may seem improbable that companies are often not aware of the need to comply with various regulations, it does happen.

Another reason that companies fail to report these breaches of regulated personal information is that they simply choose not to do so. This is because some of these companies are not compliant with even the most basic regulations and fear civil and even criminal consequences. Other companies operate in a state of regulatory confusion, complying with some regulations but not others. Many smaller companies lack consistent and focused security, legal, regulatory compliance, risk management, and privacy expertise, complicating the process of following the many requirements mandated by law.

And then there are the corporate breaches of intellectual property and trade secrets. In the majority of cases, outside of any special U.S. Department of Defense requirements or other federal reporting requirements, there is no mandate to report the breach. While legislation is circulating that would require the disclosure of certain intellectual property and trade secret thefts, this is not currently the case.

 WHAT FACTORS CREATE A PERFECT STORM?

Any number of conditions may contribute to the digital perfect storm. Here is a short, and by no means complete, list:

- Industry is vulnerable. We're not ready to meet the cyber threat, technically, organizationally, or operationally.

- The threat is expanding and intensifying.
- Legal jurisdictions often protect criminals and nation-states behind the threat.
- Government is far behind the curve and its strategy cannot adequately meet the threat.
- The global regulatory framework is inconsistent. Even within the United States, there are significant differences between states and between states and the federal government.
- Intellectual property and trade secret compromises typically do not fall under reporting guidelines, although some exceptions apply, as in the defense industry and some critical infrastructure.
- The level of awareness of the problem by executive management and boards of directors is too low.
- Companies operating on small profit margins walk a delicate balance when deciding to invest in security.
- Security is too often considered a technology issue and not an operational risk issue.
- Mobile devices are creating a highly distributed information architecture.
- Social media enables unprecedented data sharing.
- Social engineering for information access is reaching new levels and is easier to execute because of social media.
- Many companies have not adequately calculated the potential risk impact of a cyber attack that is either targeted specifically at that company or in which they are one of many enterprise victims in a broader-scale attack.
- More and more information moves offshore and to third parties.
- The insider threat continues to haunt companies, and it may get worse because we don't investigate backgrounds adequately.
- Many enterprises are in denial of their vulnerability.

Industry Vulnerability

We're not ready for cyber attacks. That's the simple truth. Think about it this way: Government regulations reflect a mandatory minimum requirement for companies to protect personally identifying information. A minimum requirement. This sets the defensive bar pretty low, although there are exceptions, including in the Commonwealth of Massachusetts, which, under the privacy regulation 201 CMR 17.0, is generally acknowledged as the most robust regulation in the United States. Still, many companies fail to meet even the low level of protection as defined by states other than Massachusetts.

And that doesn't begin to address the systems associated with critical infrastructure and proprietary corporate information. Inside many companies, the levels of awareness and compliance are low. That's not a good combination, and it promises a bad outcome in the event of attack, attacks that have come and will continue to come.

Threat Intensification

The threat range is diverse. That's part of the problem. It's not one country or one group of hackers, though China and the Russian Federation are indisputably behind the majority of attacks against U.S. targets. Nor is it just one company hacking into its competitor, or one entity described generically as "organized crime." And there is not just one reason or motive behind the attacks. While the Internet started as a simple idea, it is anything but simple today. That magnifies the problem—and the solution.

Threat intensification is reflected in the numbers, which seem almost incredible. The U.S. government reports a 17-fold increase in cyber attacks from 2009 to 2011. The U.S. Federal Emergency Management Agency reports a 650 percent increase in attacks between 2006 and 2010. It is believed that the U.S. Navy sustains some 110,000 cyber attacks every hour, about 30 attacks every second or more than 963 million a year. And that is just the U.S. Navy. The quest for global economic competitive positioning drives much of the espionage committed over the Internet. The People's Republic of China, while not the only acquirer of secrets, certainly tops the list, with its Project 863, the country's blueprint for technological and economic domination. Stealing U.S. information is a shortcut to competitive advantage. Organized criminal cyber attacks seem to be on the rise as well. Blackmailing and extorting companies is big business. Web site hijacking and associated frauds are attractive and relatively low-risk for the cyber attackers, who often hide behind the protective shield of foreign-country jurisdiction, where it remains difficult for U.S. companies to seek redress, let alone justice.

Inadequate Government Preparedness

The United States continues to advance the cyber preparedness agenda, and some very good work is going into cyber defense programs. But is it too little, too late? Better late than never, but our defenses are inadequate. Speaking at the Aspen Security Forum in 2012, General Keith B. Alexander, then chief of the National Security Agency and the head of the U.S. Cyber Command, rates U.S. cyber defense preparedness at a 3 on a scale of 1 to 10. He said that counts as an "F." So the news is not good. Consider the cyber attack history at the Department of Energy's National Nuclear Security Administration. The organization that manages the nation's nuclear stockpile is hit by as many as 10 million cyber attacks daily. Only about one-hundredth of the attacks are believed to be successful. But that still translates into about 1,000 successful attacks a day, 365,000 successful attacks a year. Ironically, the agency was created by Congress in 1999 after the Wen Ho Lee spy scandal, in which the Department of Energy was lax in its security, resulting in the loss of U.S. nuclear secrets to China.

Many smart and diligent employees of the federal government, from the National Security Agency and Department of Homeland Security to the Federal Bureau of Investigation and Central Intelligence Agency and many, many others, are working to get ahead of the threat. They are working with defense contractors, think tanks, private corporations, even other governments. But as the old Breton fisherman's prayer says, "Oh God, thy sea is so great and my boat is so small." Implied in the prayer is the theme that the challenge is fearsome, but that there is hope. Certainly this is the case. Government preparedness is low, and there's no excuse for it. The threat has been building like a tsunami for a long time. The government is acting on it as the wave is getting ready to break. But so, generally, is corporate preparedness low, and that same tsunami-like condition has been witnessed by companies, too. Yet there is hope. Perhaps the greatest hope is in achieving high levels of awareness, in government and industry—and then acting aggressively on that foundation. The time is now. Not in the next congressional session. Not in the next presidential election. Now!

Low Level of Awareness

Ignorance of the law may be no excuse for a failure to comply, but that doesn't change the discouraging and disappointing fact. Not only is there a low level of compliance with security and privacy regulations that address sensitive personal information, but there is a low awareness of the need to protect intellectual property and trade secrets. Many in government and industry are not aware of the true diversified threat to intellectual property and trade secrets. We see this frequently. When management is inadequately informed, you can be sure that awareness throughout the enterprise is low. This is a common problem even in companies (typically in smaller companies) that are bound by regulation to establish security awareness programs. These companies often lack internal (and sometimes even external) legal counsel, security officers and privacy officers, and regulatory compliance professionals. Many companies large and small also fail to properly make employees aware of the dangers of using new technologies. Mobile devices and social media are great examples.

Inadequate Risk Assessments

Many companies fail to conduct meaningful risk assessments. Oftentimes risk assessments are conducted internally by staff who lack sufficient perspective, knowledge, and experience. Or an external firm is engaged, but the lowest-cost provider resorts to a checklist approach, fails to properly scope the risk assessment, and does not test any of the controls designed to defend against constantly evolving threats. Inadequate risk assessments can be particularly dangerous because they instill a false sense of security. A false sense of security can lead to devastating consequences—and it has.

Offshoring of Data

More and more we see sensitive information sited in environments that may or may not be secure. There's inadequate vetting of security in many of these places. And often security is grossly inadequate and there are few controls in place to ensure information integrity. This is not an issue specific to regulated information. Some offshore information management companies experience high employee turnover and trade secrets disappearing with employees who move on to the next employer. Data managed offshore doesn't necessarily mean there is a higher level of risk, but it also doesn't mean there isn't. Some offshore locations establish better security than some domestic organizations. But others do not. Being able to differentiate between these two conditions is critical in the quest of sustainable information risk management through enhanced cyber security. Yet so often the distinction isn't made, and the gap widens between more secure and less secure, unarticulated, and unverified.

Insider Threat

This is a major problem, from terrorism to organized crime to competitive intelligence and corporate espionage. There are also lone wolf hackers, disenfranchised, malicious employees who steal data and sabotage data, imperiling the brand. Companies often fail to conduct good background investigations on candidates and don't reinvestigate based on factors such as life events or the passage of time. Incredibly, some companies fail to conduct any background investigations. That failure has contributed to cyber breaches that otherwise would not have occurred. There's an inherent trust of employees. We want to trust. We want to believe that our colleagues are trustworthy. But that isn't always the case. We're also broadening the definition of insiders today. Part-time employees, contractors, third-party firms, business partners all enjoy varying levels of trust—and access. Consider Edward Snowden. He worked for a third-party firm and was assigned to the U.S. National Security Agency. Whatever anyone's opinion about what Snowden has done, it's clear that there was a monumental lapse in security. And then, sometimes, background investigations are not key indicators of risk. This is what may make insiders the ultimate threat. They get our trust, in part, based on clean background checks.

Denial of Vulnerability

"It won't happen to me" is a common theme. Even though more and more cyber attack stories appear in the business and popular press, there remains a sense of disbelief among many. More than a decade ago, I wrote an *Information Security* magazine article about denial or lack of awareness at companies that think they are not going to be targeted.[2] Some executives believed then, as some do now, that they are too small, that no one knows about them. "Why would anyone attack us?" was the common refrain. I noted then that the Internet and the Web are the great democratizers of the free market. Even the smallest of organizations can appear to be—and actually are—omnipresent in a 24/7 cyber world. The World Wide Web makes companies global. I once saw a Web site representing a one-man shop in an emerging nation in Africa. He was selling to only the local market. But anyone connected to the Web had the ability to learn about his small company. Many other fledgling entities are less transparent and use the Web to transcend the trade barriers imposed by business size, reach, and scope. Of course, this is the classic double-edged sword: being visible to the market means being visible to the criminals lurking throughout the Internet. This concept escaped many businesses for a long time. Unfortunately, the myth of marginal visibility or invisibility remains entrenched in the minds of too many.

The digital threat today is as diverse as the cyber thugs, malicious insiders, nation-states, and criminal enterprises that deploy it. According to the U.S. government, more than 100 nations are engaged in technology and economic espionage. While many nations are targets of the cyber attackers in pursuit of proprietary information, the United States is target number one. The reason is straightforward. According to a Rand Corporation study, the United States leads the world in research and development, accounting for some 38 percent of the worldwide R&D spend. That's significant enough for cyber attackers to dedicate considerable resources to the task of stealing U.S. secrets.

 INCREASINGLY SOPHISTICATED ATTACKS

The risk is as multidimensional as the enterprises that do not adequately protect against it. The potential risk impact is as extensive as the virtually unlimited reach of the Internet. And the technologies that convey the attacks are far more powerful than those that placed astronauts on the moon, and so affordable that almost anyone can afford them. The total population of the world is approximately 7 billion people. Cisco Systems Inc. is forecasting that 50 billion mobile devices—just mobile devices, not desktop or even laptop computers already in the installed base by that time—will be connected to the Internet by 2020.[3] The U.S. Census Bureau forecasts that in that same year, the world population will grow to about 7.6 billion people. That's about seven mobile devices for every man, woman, and child in the world.

Cisco also reports that Android malware growth is up in 2013 over 2012 by 2,577 percent!

In 2012, we conducted an informal survey. The executives polled indicated that each one possessed at least three mobile devices, while some had four, a combination of personal devices and ones issued by their companies. We are a nation and world buried not only by information but also by the very devices that store and transmit that information. And this is still the pioneer era of mobile technology.

To the average person, the number of devices per capita may not seem to matter. But from a security, risk, and privacy perspective, it is a reflection of the amount of data that is at risk through widespread distribution. It is also an issue of how many devices may be lost or stolen, of how much data is at risk in multiple places.

MOBILE DEVICES AT HIGHER RISK

A study by the Ponemon Institute[4] clearly illustrates the mobile device concern. According to the report, large numbers of laptop computers are stolen or lost each week in U.S. airports. The total number cited in the study isn't important. It would not be unusual if the devices stolen are taken by organized criminal networks. Only the fact that portable computing devices are being stolen is new. As far back as the 1950s, airports were prime theft venues heavily penetrated by organized crime. Portable devices are stolen, targeted by criminal enterprises that understand the value of information and the fact that these units often contain vast archives of highly valuable as well as portable data. The data may be personal information or intellectual property and trade secrets, but it has value on the black market.

 ## SOMETIMES SECURITY JUST DOESN'T TAKE HOLD

On many occasions, industry's often distracted and worn-down road warriors have been observed displaying poor judgment. To some extent, it's understandable. Seated at the gate, waiting for the next flight, some secure seats close to a gate agent because they are on standby for a first-class upgrade. Typing away on their laptops, they appear industrious and engaged in writing up an expense report or maybe making a trip report, maybe a legal brief. But their ears are tuned for that magic moment when the gate agent calls their name for the upgrade and the trepidation associated with travel in the cramped and noisy economy cabin fades away. But first it's necessary to get to the gate agent before the upgrade is given to someone else. That otherwise well-meaning and maybe even cautious executive places the open laptop on the gate area seat and races to confirm the upgrade.

That's all it takes. In a fleeting moment, the laptop is gone. Worse, it is open and no password is needed to access the data. For the bad guy, it's been a good day.

In another case, an executive at a well-known firm is out of town with an associate and a client. Driving around in a rental car that evening, they opt to drop into a strip club. The executive remembers something about a security warning: Don't leave a laptop computer in the cabin of a car. If you can't take it with you (and, no, that wasn't going to happen), place the laptop in the trunk. Oh, and don't leave the keys with the valet parking attendant. So, parking the car himself, following the recommendation from the security department, he believes the computer is locked up and secure. But then he does something quite unbelievable. He places the car keys under the floor mat on the driver's side of the car and the three walk into the gentleman's club. Several hours later when they emerge, the car and the laptop are missing.

It's Friday evening, and the executive also remembers that security had advised employees that in the event of a lost or stolen laptop they should call in immediately to notify. What the executive does know is that he is going to have a hard time explaining this one, so he puts it off as long as he can. He waits until the following Monday. Bad call.

On Monday, he calls security. Security immediately sends a signal to the laptop to disable it. But from Friday night until Monday morning the laptop was not secured. And in order for the remote signal to be effective, the machine must be connected to the Internet. Unfortunately, tens if not hundreds of thousands of personal financial records are on the laptop.

Security and management have to make a tough call. Will they have to report the missing laptop to regulators? Yes. But they fail to mention the strip club, and they also state that the device is encrypted and that customer data was not exposed. But was it? Would the capture of client data, if it was exposed, result in an increase in phishing attacks and identity theft? We'll never know.

IT WASN'T ALWAYS LIKE THIS

Building a business or attacking one over the Internet rests in devices that now fit in the palm of a hand, in our laps, or on our desks. Distributing disinformation, disrupting communications and commerce, threatening critical infrastructure in a myriad of ways, waging symmetric and asymmetric information attacks, stealing information—these are the ways in which the Internet is used by criminals and nation-states. But it wasn't always that way.

Ironically, when the Internet was conceived, it was devised to be the last great hope of a successful Cold War communication between the United States and the Soviet Union, a sort of fail-safe, last-ditch effort to prevent MAD (mutual assured destruction). If nuclear war was about to be unleashed by either side, the result would be devastating. Each side assumed that the level of destruction wrought upon the other would be catastrophic, and there is little doubt that it would have been. Traditional communications might be knocked out in a preemptive strike. Or maybe the complexity of super-secure communications would not be quick enough to disengage from the process of a nuclear strike.

But the Internet had no security. In 1962, the Internet was an early-stage initiative at the Massachusetts Institute of Technology that was soon transferred to the Defense Advanced Research Projects Agency (DARPA). When the Internet came online in 1969, it was known as ARPANET, or the Advanced Research Projects Agency Network. It was the result of a private-public partnership, and perhaps one of the most telling. In those days, the Internet was four computers at four different universities. That these machines were unencumbered with security made the Internet the perfect vehicle for an emergency communication. Nothing had to be decoded or encrypted. It was brilliant in its simplicity. No suitcase with super-secret nuclear weapon launch codes always within reach of the president. Nothing to complicate or delay emergency communications with the other side. Just an immediate, simple, communication link between two heads of state when it mattered most. It was a digital lifeline, a communication link that could prevent the nuclear holocaust that all in their right mind feared. However, its simplicity was fleeting, and its accessibility has spiraled from perhaps a few dozen users to much of the world.

We have so far avoided global annihilation. The Internet has moved on. Ironically, its complete lack of security during the Cold War has led to the quest for continuously improved security.

 ## WITHOUT A BANG

The meeting point between the nuclear age and the digital age arrived, fortunately, without a bang. But neither was the arrival heralded with a whimper; it was more like an alarm bell, a warning before the next storm. The technology trail was clear, especially in retrospect:

- Information would multiply.
- Computers would become more powerful, yet smaller, and more ubiquitous than anyone could have imagined.
- They would hold increasingly large amounts of information.
- The Internet would keep expanding, moving more and more information at faster and faster speeds.
- Computers would also become less and less expensive.
- More people would have more information stored on more computing devices.
- Cyber security was slow to catch up—and still is.

The days of social media, mobile devices, and Internet everywhere and all of the time were still ahead of us. Of course, security failed to keep pace with the technology race. Many technologists believed that all information should be accessible to all, shared by anyone and everyone. Those who believed security was essential fell behind the curve that became the tsunami of the information age and the information superhighway. This led to companies and government adopting technology at a dizzying pace. The purchase of information technology was tied inextricably to increasing performance associated with creating, moving, and storing increasingly massive volumes of data. It was the evolving Big Data of yesterday. But like all tsunamis, one of two eventualities occurs: It either peters out or it crashes down on the inadequately prepared and the unaware, wreaking havoc.

Security, then, was an afterthought. This led to a problem: Technology adoption was based on issues other than the defense of information. There was a huge gap between performance and security as elements of consideration in the adoption and integration of technology. It seems hard to believe today, but it was true. Security got in the way.

We are witness to an information explosion. A lot of the information is in the form of e-mail. In May 2013, the web site the Culture-ist (www .thecultureist.com) posted some interesting statistics about the Internet and its use. Nearly two and a half billion people, or some 37.3 percent of the planet's population, use the Internet, approximately 70 percent of them on a daily basis. This translates into about 144 billion e-mails every day. But here's the problem: Nearly 70 percent of the e-mails are not to and from friends and business colleagues. These roughly 99 billion daily e-mails are spam (mostly advertisements) coming from around the world, many of them infected with viruses in an attempt to gain access to computers and compromise information integrity.

 ## A BOARD ISSUE

This book is an attempt to raise the level of awareness about the cyber threat and what to do about it. The cyber threat is a board of directors' issue. Yet when some senior executives and board members hear the word "security" or "technology," there's a disconnect. They think it's not their issue. Let the technology people deal with it. Let the security people deal with it. Although there is evidence that this perception is changing, we have a long way to go. The word "cyber," they're starting to get.

For several years I had the opportunity to travel around the country, addressing information security officers in a number of cities. Over that period I met with perhaps a couple of thousand security professionals. From one city to the next, a common theme became apparent. In most every venue, at the conclusion of a presentation there was the opportunity for these professionals to ask questions or make comments. The most consistent comment was something like this: "No one in upper management at my company seems to care about security. If I mention a security issue, they sort of roll their eyes and refer me to somebody else, usually somebody lower in the organization. What should I do?" Clearly, many of these professionals were looking for support. My recommendation was this: Internal audit and legal should always be interested in any security concerns. But that's not always the case.

Stephen Burns and David Marston of the National Security Institute have addressed the issue of how to get people interested in information security. "Here's an age-old security riddle: How do you get people in the workplace to pay attention to information security? Answer: Make it personal and tell them what's in it for them." The question may then be asked: How do you get the board of directors and executive management interested in information security? The answer is much the same. Make it personal and tell them what's in it for them. Effectively managing risk is personal. Information security is personal. We don't always interpret it that way, but it is.

The chief information security officer (CISO), in tandem with others, will have to create this momentum, along with the general counsel, chief risk officers, and others. "The focus of information security and cyber risk management is heading in the right direction," according to M. J. Vaidya, CISO for Americas at General Motors and an adjunct professor at New York University's School of Engineering. "The role of the CISO is clearly changing and growing," he says. "The CISOs of today have to embrace ambiguity, focus on risk, build relationships throughout the organization, gather intelligence, and consistently innovate."

 ## THE CYBER FRANKENSTEIN COMETH

Managing the cyber threat and resulting cyber risk results in increased competitiveness, enhanced value, the creation of exploitable opportunity, and economic advantage. The cyber threat is not unique. It is manageable; its impact can be mitigated. We have created the cyber Frankenstein monster of our day, but we can deal with it. What we cannot do is ignore it. We cannot pretend that it is "a technical thing," as many do, and thereby relegate discussions of it to a technical team. Yes, it does involve technology, which scares a lot of people, among them nontechnical board members and senior management. We've got to move beyond that, and we've got to do it now. The message is getting out there, but not fast enough. The cyber threat is accelerating faster than we seem capable of managing it. But that's got to change.

We have identified this monster, this perfect storm. There's no going back. We know what all the elements of it look like. We know what powers it, and we know how it materializes and how it impacts organizations large and small, private and public, regulated and unregulated, foreign and domestic. Where we have perhaps failed is in our ability to organize against the threat, to organize our thinking about the consequences of inaction, to coordinate our defenses, and to invest in the ability to better manage and defeat the threat.

Managing information has been perceived as a productivity issue. In reality, managing information in a fashion that does not increase personal and institutional risk is the issue. We have placed our feet into the waters of a new wave of how information will be managed. It is subject to this perfect storm. How we engage the future of information management will be a principal determinant of how we will define success.

Information is value. Companies build value, which is based on the integrity of their information. Value defines success. Success builds the foundation for sustainability, and there is no sustainability without value. Sustainable value must be the wheel that turns the ship to face this perfect storm head-on. This requires managing cyber risk, and right now there's not much to brag about in how that risk is being managed.

 DEFINING SUCCESS

I will consider this book a success if it brings boards and executive management one step closer to bridging the communications gulf that separates the defenders of information and the defenders of corporate value. Both groups are working toward the same conclusion. Independently they are working to sustain integrity. They just don't speak the same language and they take different paths, but all paths are not created equal. And in failing to speak the same language they fail to be adequately prepared to face the challenges that all of us face today and will continue to face well into the future.

A question that is often asked in executive social media forums is, "What do you say when the CEO asks, 'Are we secure?'" Too often, the answer does not match the reality.

 NOTES

1. "Barbarians at the Digital Gate," *Wall Street Journal*, February 5, 2013.
2. MacDonnell Ulsch, "The Forest for the Trees," *Information Security*, June 2000.
3. Cisco Systems Inc., "The Internet of Things," http://share.cisco.com/internet-of-things.html.
4. Ponemon Institute, "Global Study on Mobility Risks," February 2012, http://www.ponemon.org/local/upload/file/Websense_Mobility_US_Final.pdf.

PART I

The Cyber Threat to the Corporate Brand

How It Will Impact Your Company

CHAPTER ONE

The Rise of Cyber Organized Crime and Its Global Impact

> The infectiousness of crime is like that of the plague.
>
> —*Napoleon Bonaparte*

W HAT IS the *cyber threat?* The most basic definition is uncommonly simple: It is that common ground where human beings, the Internet, and computers interact. The resulting threat can be an honest mistake—or a malicious strike. An honest mistake can be addressed through increased awareness about the importance of handling sensitive information. The malicious strike is different.

The crime wave of the future is here: the growing criminal conspiracy known as transnational organized crime, or TOC. Criminal networks and organized groups work throughout multiple countries to plan and execute their business goals. Their operations involve many of the most despicable of crimes: human trafficking, the sexual exploitation of adults and children, narcotics trafficking, violent crimes, corruption, arms trafficking, and even the selling of human body parts and endangered species. Unfortunately, TOC is an early adopter of new technology and strong security.

Transnational organized crime is somewhat fluidly defined by the United Nations as "offences committed in more than one State" and "those that take place in one State but are planned or controlled in another. Also included are crimes in one State committed by groups that operate in more than one State, and crimes committed in one State that has substantial effects in another State."[1]

Transnational cyber crime is believed to have defrauded U.S. companies and citizens of billions of dollars a year, according to some reports. Others believe the amount is far higher. The amount of financial loss is extremely hard to gauge and is subject to interpretation by varying experts. But the following is a fact: Regardless of the actual numbers, this is a serious and growing problem. And this is just an example of a series of crimes perpetrated by the online frauds practiced by Eastern European cyber crime networks and does not include frauds from other regions of the globe, such as the People's Republic of China.

The UN notes that "transnational organized crime manifests in many forms, including as trafficking in drugs, firearms and even persons . . . and undermine financial systems through money laundering. The vast sums of money involved can compromise legitimate economies."[2]

Most law enforcement organizations, as well as the UN Office on Drugs and Crime (UNODC), acknowledge that organized crime has grown dramatically and has become a truly global issue. "Transnational organized crime can permeate government agencies and institutions, infiltrating business and politics, and hindering economic and social development," says the UN, which also states that transnational organized crime is "undermining governance and democracy by empowering those who operate outside the law."[3]

As the name suggests, transnational crime knows no borders, geographical or ethical. While such criminal behavior is global, covering virtually every continent, a few trends have become clear. Narcotics drive a lot of organized criminal behavior, and so do child pornography, prostitution, human trafficking, and gambling. No country seems immune, with a few possible exceptions. But Russian organized crime, and then Eastern European organized crime, has grown rapidly. With the so-called democratization of Russia came the liberation of organized crime, which under the Soviet Union had largely been contained and controlled by the KGB, ironically the state security apparatus. And then came the integration of technology. Transnational crime has embraced technology and security with a fervor that even many major corporations have not.

In Russia, for example, there has been an increase in legislative action to combat cyber crime originating there. But while there may be the legislative will to fight cyber crime, it seems that no real impact has been made in reducing it, at least not yet. In the pursuit of civil and criminal justice in many cyber crimes originating in, or intimately involving, Russia, that nation has proved less than helpful. Seeking cooperation from ISPs in the region, for example, is an often slow and painful process. Part of the reason for the lack of momentum in cooperation is that much of the cyber crime originates not only in Russia but in the Ukraine and other former Soviet bloc nations. It does not help that U.S.-Russia relations have become increasingly strained over Russia's grant of temporary asylum to U.S. National Security Agency whistleblower Edward Snowden, and it remains uncertain what impact Russia's dispute with Ukraine—and potentially other former Soviet states—will have on organized crime in the future. However, history suggests that not much is likely to change, at least not change for the better.

Ironically, one important distinction that separates legitimate businesses from criminal groups is the widespread and consistent use of encryption. Many companies see encryption as a distraction, an impediment that is counter to information management and productivity. "It's complicated, it slows things down," businesses often say. "It requires a lot of management." But criminal groups take a more reasoned view and understand that it creates a more protected channel of communications than those used by many companies, despite the fact that law enforcement is making gains in penetrating encrypted networks.

Organized cyber crime on a global scale enjoys several conditions that make it extremely difficult to combat. These include the following:

- Organized crime invests heavily in technology and knows how to use it. They're early adopters.
- Organized crime uses encryption aggressively, unlike many companies around the world. Criminals understand the value of using strong encryption as a method of secure communication and seems to worry less about the technical and administrative costs associated with it. While U.S. companies managing regulated data do use some encryption, even many regulations do not actually mandate the use of it, and then some companies that are supposed to encrypt information do not.
- Since most intellectual property and trade secret protection is not mandated by law, or by boards of directors, encryption often is not used to defend this information, regardless of its financial value.

- Organized crime uses something called Tor, or The Onion Router. Tor is a series of encrypted networks that are optimally secure and slow or block law enforcement investigations, although law enforcement is making progress in breaking these communications systems.
- Organized crime internal policy enforcement is very strict, and often lethal.
- The low cost of technology enables the acquisition of extremely powerful technology, even in mobile platforms.
- The expansive use of social media creates new opportunities for the acquisition of information useful in profiling identity theft and phishing targets.
- Criminals skillfully cover their tracks during a breach. In targeted companies with inadequate security defenses, the attackers are largely able to enter and exit, undiscovered, with relative ease. Some attackers have been identified only after careful review of the electronic log information, from firewalls, for example. But in many cases these logs are not reviewed regularly or even often, so the attack may not become apparent until the logs come under review. In companies without strong defenses and disciplined review policies, attacks can go on for long periods of time.
- Organized crime has no moderating moral compass, and, conversely, most law enforcement agencies abide by a strict set of guidelines, creating a gap between criminal action and apprehension. This is particularly true when the targeted entities are based outside the region where the criminal enterprises are based. Human trafficking and exploitation are accepted as legitimate forms of business.
- Marginally effective or even ineffective laws governing jurisdiction become obstructions in the investigative process. The global legal framework for combating cyber crime is woefully deficient.

Cyber crime and money laundering are widespread in TOC. The reason is simple: These crimes are profitable. All of the crimes noted, especially in emerging nations, generate significant revenue. But unlike normal businesses, criminal organizations often do not use traditional banks. They are more apt to use money-laundering services such as Liberty Reserve, S.A., which is said by U.S. law enforcement authorities to have specialized in servicing organized criminal networks.

Transnational criminal networks engage in a variety of cyber crimes. The cost to business and to consumers runs into the billions of dollars a year. Perhaps most significantly, these operations could undermine confidence in the global financial system.

IS NOTHING SACRED?

Over a cup of coffee one spring afternoon in the heart of Boston's Financial District, an attorney and veteran insurance industry executive with 30 years of experience put it succinctly. "When you get labeled with child pornography, that's the worst-case scenario. How do you ever come back from that? You get branded with the label of being associated with child pornography, and that's it. You can kiss your career good-bye."

He posed an interesting question. It used to be that the subject of child pornography never saw the light of day, at least not among respectable adults, except law enforcement. But this seems to be a troubling corner around which we have turned, thanks to organized crime, which has the dubious and disgusting distinction of controlling much of that despicable content.

Another attorney, a former U.S. Justice Department official, attended a meeting in Washington, D.C., in which photographs of children engaged in sexual acts with adults were spread across the table. He threw up. He had passed the test. Child pornography disgusted him to the point of nausea. He would now join the task force formed to combat the sexual abuse of minors. Human smuggling is an equally appalling crime and is associated with transnational organized crime.

Disturbingly, an increasing number of data breaches involve either actual photographic, morphed, or textual references to child trafficking and sexual exploitation. The intent is often to extort money, blackmail, compromise corporate brands, and steal proprietary information. It seems that the criminals behind these crimes will stop at nothing to devise extortion and blackmail schemes. Using the Internet for exploitation has become commonplace.

According to the White House, human trafficking is linked to other transnational crimes that include "drug trafficking and the corruption of government officials. [Traffickers] can move criminals, fugitives, terrorists, and trafficking victims, as well as economic migrants. They undermine the sovereignty of nations and often endanger the lives of those being smuggled."

In its 2010 report *The Globalization of Crime: A Transnational Organized Crime Threat Assessment*, the UNODC estimated that the smuggling of persons from Latin America to the United States generated approximately $6.6 billion annually in illicit proceeds for human smuggling networks.[4]

The connection to cyber crime is, among other things, money laundering. Criminal proceeds must be laundered. The Internet and the Web have become tools used by money launderers. The offshore company known as Liberty

Reserve was shut down by U.S. law enforcement and charged with a number of financial crimes for laundering the assets of criminal organizations around the world.

In written testimony before the House Committee on Appropriations Subcommittee on Homeland Security hearing on the president's fiscal year 2013 budget request for the Secret Service, Director Mark J. Sullivan remarked that "threats posed by cyber criminals to our nation's payment and financial systems . . . are a growing concern to the Secret Service."[5] The director stated that among the Secret Service's top priorities are "safeguarding and securing cyber space; and preventing cyber crime and other malicious uses of cyber space. . . . The Secret Service's Cyber Intelligence Section manages three cyber crime working groups that work to identify, locate, and apprehend transnational cyber criminals involved in network intrusions, hacking attacks, malware development, phishing schemes, and other forms of cyber crime."

Transnational cyber crime is complex to break. Data and criminals move at will across national boundaries. While investigating these crimes can be challenging, it's not impossible.

 ## THE LIBERTY RESERVE CASE: MONEY LAUNDERING IN THE DIGITAL AGE

Consider the Liberty Reserve case. "These arrests are an example of the Secret Service's commitment to investigate and apprehend criminals engaged in the misuse of virtual currencies to conduct global monetary fraud," says Steven G. Hughes, special agent in charge of the U.S. Secret Service New York Field Office. "Cyber criminals should be reminded today that they are unable to hide behind the anonymity of the Internet to avoid regulated financial systems."

Federal prosecutors point to Liberty Reserve as a major player in cyber crime. "Liberty Reserve has emerged as one of the principal means by which cyber criminals around the world distribute, store, and launder proceeds of their illegal activity."[6] It was believed to have become the "financial hub of the cyber-crime world, facilitating a broad range of online criminal activity, including credit card fraud, computer hacking, child pornography, and narcotics trafficking." Simply put, Liberty Reserve helped a lot of transnational criminal organizations launder ill-gotten gains. The U.S. government called the scope of the defendants' unlawful conduct "staggering." It was also a tangled web.

Here is how Liberty Reserve operated. According to the indictment, Liberty Reserve was "used extensively for illegal purposes, functioning, in effect as the bank of choice for the criminal underworld." Liberty Reserve users are said to have routinely established accounts under false names. Prosecutors will argue in court that Liberty Reserve users believed that the veil of anonymity created and deployed by Liberty Reserve would protect them with impunity.

And for a while, it did.

The Liberty Reserve case has affected a number of U.S. companies that were targeted for a variety of Web-related frauds, including blackmail and extortion. The Secret Service, the Department of Homeland Security, and the Internal Revenue Service executed arrest and search warrants in seven countries, including Spain, Costa Rica, the Netherlands, and the United States. Assets of Liberty Reserve were frozen in Hong Kong, Spain, Morocco, and China. Current and former executives of Liberty Reserve were charged with violating numerous anti–money laundering statutes and operating as illegal money transmitters.

According to the Treasury Department, Liberty Reserve developed a virtual currency called "LR" that was used to anonymously buy and sell software designed to steal personal information and attack financial institutions. The hackers who in 2013 stole $45 million from two Middle Eastern banks by hacking prepaid debit cards used Liberty Reserve to distribute the proceeds of the crime.

Liberty Reserve's criminal conduct was as widespread as it was lucrative. It had approximately 1 million users worldwide, with more than 200,000 in the United States. It is estimated that Liberty Reserve processed more than 12 million financial transactions annually, with a combined value of more than $1.4 billion. From 2006 to May 2013, it is believed that Liberty Reserve, according to the Secret Service, processed an estimated 55 million separate financial transactions and laundered more than $6 billion in criminal proceeds.

The U.S. Department of the Treasury, using the USA Patriot Act, said of Liberty Reserve that it was "specifically designed and frequently used to facilitate money laundering in cyber space."

A grand jury indictment filed in U.S. District Court for the Southern District of New York lays out a number of details about Liberty Reserve and the crimes it is alleged to have committed. The indictment describes in detail the financial frauds committed by Liberty Reserve defendants, including the development of a system of payments that allowed users to open accounts under false names in order to conceal criminal activity. Users opened accounts under false names such as "Russia Hackers" and "Hacker Account."

Here is how the money-laundering scheme worked:

A user first had to open an account through the Liberty Reserve web site. Users did so using only a name, address, and date of birth. Liberty Reserve is said not to have made any attempt to verify any account holder information through the examination of identification documents or even a credit card. This was tantamount to an open invitation to criminal use for money-laundering purposes. Accounts could be opened using fictitious information.

Once an account was opened, the user could conduct business anonymously with any other Liberty Reserve users, a group of unidentified and undocumented individuals. Liberty Reserve charged a 1 percent fee every time a user transferred the LR digital currency through the Liberty Reserve system. Users could opt to include what was called a "privacy fee" of 75 cents per transaction that enabled users to hide account numbers, adding an additional layer of anonymity and making the transaction virtually untraceable.

But Liberty Reserve added another layer of anonymity. It did not allow users to deposit money directly into their accounts by issuing a credit card payment, for example, or by wire transfer. Users were not allowed to withdraw funds from Liberty Reserve, so no ATM withdrawals, for example. Users were required to make deposits and withdrawals through third-party operations known as "exchangers." This enabled Liberty Reserve to avoid collecting any user data through banking transactions or other activity that would leave a centralized financial paper trail.

Liberty Reserve's exchangers were third parties who maintained direct relationships with the company. They bought and sold LRs in bulk in exchange for conventional currency. Then they bought and sold LRs in smaller transactions with end users in exchange for conventional currency. So in order to fund a Liberty Reserve account, a user was required to transmit conventional currency to an exchanger. When the exchanger received the user's payment, the exchanger credited the user's Liberty Reserve account with a corresponding amount of LR, by transferring LR from the exchanger's Liberty Reserve account to the user's Liberty Reserve account.

If a Liberty Reserve user wanted to withdraw funds from the Liberty Reserve account, the user was required to transfer LRs from the Liberty Reserve account to an exchanger's Liberty Reserve account, and then the exchanger made arrangements to provide the user a corresponding amount of mainstream currency.

Liberty Reserve's web site, taken down by U.S. law enforcement in May 2013, recommended a number of what it labeled at the time as "preapproved" exchangers. Of course, consistent with the fraud, the exchangers tended to be unlicensed money-transmitting businesses operating without meaningful government oversight or regulation, in nations not well known for financial transaction oversight and regulation. The exchangers listed by Liberty Reserve were concentrated mostly in Malaysia, Russia, Nigeria, and Vietnam.

THE CORRUPTION FACTOR

Government corruption is always a factor when it comes to trusted transactions, ones subject to close scrutiny, and where the interests of law enforcement, consumers' rights, and information integrity are enforced. Interestingly, each of the nations noted above that hosted the exchangers recommended by Liberty Reserve received poor ratings on the Transparency International Corruption Perceptions Index of 2012. The index scores countries on a scale of 0 to 100. A zero score means that a country is perceived to be highly corrupt, while a score of 100 means that a country is perceived to be free of corruption. No country received a score of 100, though some rated very highly.

According to the index, about two-thirds of countries scored below 50, "indicating a serious corruption problem." Transnational criminal factions are often attracted to the lower-scoring nations, where corruption and bribery are more common and where governments are more likely to look the other way, many times even participating in illicit activity themselves.

Russia, for example, one of the countries hosting unlicensed money transmitters, received a score of 28 and was ranked 133 out of 174 countries in lack of corruption. For perspective, consider that nations also receiving a score of 28 and a ranking of 133 included Comoros, Guyana, Honduras, Iran, and Kazakhstan. Nigeria, another host country, ranked 139 of 174, with a score of 27. Vietnam, with a score of 31, was ranked 123. Malaysia was ranked higher, at 54, and its score was 49, the same as the Czech Republic and Latvia. Costa Rica, the former host country to Liberty Reserve, was ranked 48 and scored 54. By comparison, Denmark and Finland (both scored 90) were perceived as the least corrupt, followed by New Zealand, Singapore, Switzerland, and Australia. The United States was ranked 19 and scored 73, while Canada received a rank of ninth and scored 84.

The Liberty Reserve–recommended exchangers, not surprisingly, charged transaction fees for their services. Typically the fee would be 5 percent or even more of the transaction value, much higher than a legitimate bank or payment processor would charge for the same service. Clearly, the Liberty Reserve system was designed "so that criminals could effect financial transactions under multiple layers of anonymity and thereby avoid apprehension by law enforcement," according to court records.

Liberty Reserve's web site featured a shopping cart feature, similar to most any transactional web site. So-called merchant web sites used this feature to accept LR digital currency as a form of payment. These "merchants" were, according to prosecutors, overwhelmingly criminal in nature. The criminal actions included "traffickers of stolen credit card data and personal identity information; peddlers of various types of online Ponzi schemes; computer hackers for hire; unregulated gambling enterprises; and underground drug-dealing web sites." But the criminal activity did not stop there. Liberty Reserve was also used by "cyber criminals to launder criminal proceeds and transfer funds among criminal associates. The company was used by credit card theft rings and computer hacking operating in countries around the world, including Vietnam, Nigeria, Hong Kong, China, and the U.S."

Not mentioned in the court documents was a case in which a Costa Rican national came to the United States, worked for a company there, gained access to consumer credit cards, and sold them to criminal gangs operating in the United States and Costa Rica. It is believed that the proceeds from the credit cards were laundered through Liberty Reserve.

Liberty Reserve defendants knew that the U.S. government was breathing down their necks. In fact, U.S. law enforcement was able to capture an online chat between two defendants. The chat shows that Liberty Reserve was on the law enforcement radar screen: "Everyone in the USA," such as "DOJ [Department of Justice]," knows that "LR is a [a] money laundering operation that hackers use."

In 2009 the company applied for a license to operate out of Costa Rica, but the application was denied, for a very simple reason: Liberty Reserve, according to Costa Rican authorities, lacked even the most basic anti–money laundering controls, such as the one called "know your customer," or KYC. This is especially important as a defense for financial institutions. U.S. regulations refer to it as a Customer Identification Program, or CIP, and one of its goals is to be able to anticipate the likelihood of a customer's engagement in money laundering.

The USA Patriot Act requires that financial institutions "shall establish appropriate, specific, and, where necessary, enhanced, due diligence policies, procedures, and controls that are reasonably designed to detect and report instances of money laundering through those accounts."[7] Not only did Liberty Reserve fail to observe the KYC requirement, but the company also had no effective means of tracking suspicious activity. Of course, it appears that Liberty Reserve had no incentive or desire to track suspicious activity, because seemingly the overwhelming majority of its transactions were suspicious.

If the company had been a legitimate entity, it would have made some attempt to remedy its anti–money laundering deficiencies. Instead, it created a deception. Liberty Reserve "created a system designed to feign compliance with anti–money laundering procedures," according to court records. The defendants, in effect buying more time in which to continue their illicit operations, "created a computer portal that appeared to give Costa Rican regulators the ability to access Liberty Reserve transactional information and monitor it for suspicious activity." In fact it was a ruse. Most of the data in the portal was planted by the company; it was mostly false. The falsified data could be manipulated and serve as a veil to conceal information that Liberty Reserve did not want regulators to see.

By November 2011 the company was still unable to obtain a license to operate legally in Costa Rica. During that time the U.S. Treasury Department's Financial Crimes Enforcement Network (FinCEN) took notice. The U.S. government began to notify financial institutions of the risk of doing business with Liberty Reserve. In part, the notification stated, there was a "risk associated with providing financial services to Liberty Reserve. . . . Information obtained by the United States Department of the Treasury indicates Liberty Reserve is . . . currently being used by criminals to conduct anonymous transactions to move money globally."

In a move of deception, about two weeks after the FinCEN notice the defendants told Costa Rican authorities that the business had been sold to a foreign company and would no longer be operating in Costa Rica. But that was not the case. It just withdrew its application for a money-transmitting license, suggesting that it had shut down its office there. Of course, Liberty Reserve continued to operate out of Costa Rica. It went underground and used a scaled-down office, working out of facilities held in the name of shell companies controlled by one of the defendants.

The misrepresentations didn't end there. At about the same time, the defendants were emptying Liberty Reserve bank accounts in Costa Rica of millions of dollars. According to the indictment, the monies were transferred first to a bank account in Cyprus held in the name of a shell company controlled by several of the Liberty Reserve defendants, and then to a bank account in Russia in the name of another shell company.

Soon after Liberty Reserve moved to empty its bank accounts, U.S. law enforcement authorities requested that the Costa Rican government move against the Liberty Reserve accounts. Costa Rica seized about $19.5 million. In response to the seizure, the defendants took another evasive action against more seizures by moving Liberty Reserve funds into more than two dozen shell companies' accounts in Cyprus, Hong Kong, China, Morocco, Australia, and Spain.

Prosecutors have charged that the defendants knew that the money they were laundering was the result of unlawful activity: identity theft, access device fraud, computer hacking, wire fraud, child pornography, and narcotics trafficking.

It is important to remember that the application was filed in 2009 and that the company was not taken down by U.S. law enforcement until May 2013. So for more than three years after the application was denied, Liberty Reserve continued to operate. The point is this: Every company must rely on its own risk management and due diligence process. Law enforcement and prosecutorial action require varying but significant time for evidence collection and case development. This is especially true in transnational crime, conflicting laws, and geopolitical considerations. So even when a corrupt company has come under the close examination of federal authorities and advisories have been sent to financial firms as a warning, the continued operation of the criminal company poses a significant threat to any enterprise that drifts into its scope or is targeted by it.

Although not specified in the indictment, some of the illicit financial proceeds handled by Liberty Reserve involved the theft and unauthorized use of corporate intellectual property by criminal networks around the world. The use of compromised intellectual property was involved in the commission of identity theft and financial fraud, through the deployment of scam web sites. The web sites looked valid. And that's the point. Because the web sites looked authentic, potential investors and other high net worth individuals and executives would visit them and open an account "to receive additional information." To open an informational account, the site visitor would simply create a login ID and a password.

Such sites typically work in the following way: Once a prospective investor reads the sales pitch, they have the option to learn more. Potential investors are often high net worth executives who possess discretionary income available for investment. The investor has the option to learn more by establishing a no-obligation account, created by entering login identification and a password. The problem, one anticipated by the organized criminals, is that many visitors will use their corporate e-mail address as the login ID and their corporate e-mail password. The visitor will assume that the password, because it does not display on the screen in clear text, is secure. In fact, it is not. So in registering for an informational account, the visitor has just handed over to criminals around the world four critical pieces of information to be used later:

1. The name of the visitor;
2. The name of the company;
3. The prominence of the company (established, well-known brands, for example); and
4. A password.

The site visitor, having unwittingly surrendered critical confidential information, is now at elevated risk, and so is the company. The visitor could be targeted for specialized attacks to defraud him. But the data could also be used to try to gain access to proprietary data belonging to the company. With the individual's secret login credentials, depending on other security measures in place at the company, the criminals may gain access to privileged information, including valuable trade secrets, even the individual's financial accounts. Additionally, these individuals' profiles could be used to create and proliferate additional fraudulent investment sites.

There are cases where extensive financial account information on executives has been stolen from financial institutions and posted online by criminals in order to intimidate the targeted executive. Once the corporate and executive brand data is distributed by the franchisees across the Web and plastered on unsavory web sites containing references to human trafficking, sexual exploitation, and other crimes, the criminals know that the executive and the company are under a lot of stress. They know that law enforcement will be brought in, and they know that the targeted company is going to be very sensitive to the negative exploitation of its brand and its executives. They keep putting pressure on the company by spreading its information to more and more exploitative web sites around the world.

So the web site is up, running, and proliferating: It is set to generate revenue from the franchises. The number of operators of the scam helps slow down law enforcement. Sometimes the criminal groups offshore will coordinate an up-close-and-personal component of an attack. They will have a contact close to the target company positioned within wireless broadcast range and provide a provocative name to the wireless network. If an employee at the target company clicks on the link, malware transmitted to the environment, unless it is identified and disabled, may broadcast data back to the criminal organization.

Once the corporation and its management and board have been victimized in this multifaceted fashion, the company is likely to start getting extortion demands: Buy the rogue web site to stop the attack and defamation. But of course, the attacks and defamation never stop, especially where franchised scam web sites continue the assault.

In addition to Liberty Reserve, at least one of the defendants in the case was also running companies named Silverhand Solutions & Technology, Worldwide E-Commerce Business, Grufo Lulu Limitado, Triton Group, Gold Age Inc., and Cyberfuel.com. These companies are assumed to have been engaged in various money-laundering activities. Any legitimate company that used the services of any of these brands should investigate the transactions to determine any potential risk.

INFORMATION THREAT, PHYSICAL THREAT

Being attacked by organized crime is always serious business. While many attacks originate in foreign countries, there is always the risk that local criminal affiliates engaged in transnational crime may become involved in extortion schemes, as has been discussed. Clients often ask about the potential physical threat against senior executives and their families. Some targeted executives acquire kidnapping insurance and hire executive protection firms to guard against the threat, and they may also want to understand the degree of physical security protection at their companies.

While many companies have successfully integrated physical, logical, and administrative security, many others have not. Physical security is often lax. When the executive team understands that their firm has been targeted and that organized crime may be behind the breach, the perception changes. Security takes on a new meaning. It is not a stretch to suggest that transnational crime is going to grow, and that cyber crimes will increasingly involve proximity, especially given the widespread use of wireless networks and corporate vulnerabilities.

As the old saying goes, better safe than sorry. When criminals attack the corporate brand, it goes without saying that they will do whatever they deem necessary to defraud and extort companies. This may mean disclosing an executive's home address and family members' names as a form of intimidation.

It may mean showing up outside the corporate headquarters and broadcasting a wireless network in an attempt to get employees to log in and thereby allow for the downloading of malware. Criminals may e-mail the targeted executive with extortion demands. They may even threaten that executive. Law enforcement cannot be depended on to protect every executive targeted by criminals. Every company should practice good security and the management of risk. The time to develop a robust response plan is not after the extortion demand is made.

Tomas Filipiak, an information security consultant and information warfare officer who served as a U.S. Army captain, observed, "Instead of proactive leadership, information security awareness has been implemented as a reaction to unfortunate events such as government and corporate espionage and identity theft. The trend of reactionary vulnerability remediation is an effect of the natural challenge of establishing return on investment metrics for security. The high cost of information security measures coupled with tight budgets may tempt leadership to reduce security expenditures, especially if a high-profile incident hasn't occurred in the recent past."[8]

He continues, "Enemies that choose to engage in cyber warfare to attack our national interests or steal information are patient. They can see the trend in reactionary measures, and if they are smart they will wait for calm to relax our vigilance and our information security budgets. With our defenses weakened, they would be empowered to strike utilizing zero day attacks that may have not been considered or for which defensive measures have proved to be cost-prohibitive. Zero day attacks are simply ones that have not yet been addressed by those developing patches or fixes to stop the attacks. Certainly there will be a response to such an attack, but what collateral damage will need to be overcome that could have been prevented with proactive information security awareness measures?"

 NOTES

1. United Nations Office on Drugs and Crime, "Organized Crime," https://www.unodc.org/unodc/en/organized-crime/index.html.
2. Ibid.
3. Ibid.
4. Ibid.
5. House of Representatives, Committee on Homeland Security, "Subcommittee Hearing: United States Secret Service: Examining Protective and Investigative

Missions and Challenges in 2012," September 14, 2011, http://homeland .house.gov/hearing/subcommittee-hearing-united-states-secret-service-examining-protective-and-investigative.
6. Liberty Reserve Grand Jury Indictment, United States District Court, Southern District of New York, May 2013.
7. Ibid.
8. Author conversation with Tomas Filipiak, October 2013.

CHAPTER TWO

The Emergence of the Cyber Nation-State and Technology Espionage

Red China Rising and Its Global Cyber Theft Strategy

There, is a sleeping giant. Let him sleep! If he awakes, he will shake the world.

—*Napoleon on China*

M AKE NO mistake: China is wide awake. Its quest for the proprietary information developed by others, principally the United States, is aggressive, unrelenting, sophisticated, structured, supported by the government and its military, and, ultimately, successful. And China denies it.

Is China alone in its quest for information? Of course not. A lot of people, nations, and companies steal information that does not belong to them. The art of industrial, economic, and technology espionage has a long history. Sometimes employees steal information. Sometimes terrorist groups are in on the action. Social protest groups are known to have stolen proprietary information. Certainly criminal organizations steal information. Information has value, financial as well as strategic, military, economic, diplomatic, cultural, political, and social. Information is, as has been said, power. It is also the potential or the promise of power.

At a very simplistic level, China's cyber strategy is very unambiguous. It wants to acquire in any way it can as much useful information as it can. But what's important from China's point of view? In part, what is important to China now is what is important to China's future. Again, simplistically, China is stealing targeted information that is part of a larger strategic plan to possess a wide range of the technologies that will enhance its competitive positioning globally. Acquiring this information from other countries, mostly from the United States, lowers its cost of research and development and shortens its time to market. Going to market with competitive pricing, enabled through illicit acquisition, has diplomatic as well as economic implications for China. It gives China the power of enhanced market presence and market share, which translates into diplomatic advantage and the power of political persuasion through economic leverage.

The People's Republic of China is at the forefront of nation-state espionage, despite its ongoing denials for decades. But the theft of U.S. technological secrets by China is not new. Its espionage program, Project 863, was developed in 1986 as the State High-Tech Research and Development Plan. That plan is China's evolving blueprint for technological independence and global economic empowerment.

In 1986, four Chinese scientists proposed to accelerate the communist country's high-technology sector development, with China realizing that the way to a sustainable global market was not in supplying its own population with new technologies but in delivering quality products and services based on competitively priced technologies that would drive the economic future of consuming and emerging nations. And so Project 863 was born, named for its date of inception, March (the third month) 1986. It received the personal approval of Deng Xiaoping, who as Chinese head of state from 1978 to 1992 moved the country toward a market-based economy. He knew this would require a formidable change and that China did not possess the fundamental technologies that it needed to compete in a technologically driven world.

China has even stated publicly in its State High-Tech Research and Development Plan the goal of Project or Program 863: "Objectives of this program during the 10th Five-year Plan are to boost innovation capacity in the high-tech sectors, particularly in strategic high-tech fields, in order to gain a foothold in the world arena; to strive to achieve breakthroughs in key technical fields that concern the national economic lifeline and national security; and to achieve 'leap-frog' development in key high-tech fields in which China enjoys relative advantages or should take strategic positions in order to provide high-tech support to fulfill strategic objectives in the implementation of the third step of our modernization process."[1]

It is no secret that China has long been a benefactor of the ongoing development of U.S. technology. The Rand Corporation places U.S. research and development expenditures as approximately 38 percent of the world total. This makes an attractive, consolidated target. For decades, China has been acquiring proprietary intellectual property, often through academic and industry conferences, fertile ground for identifying cutting-edge technologies. Another common method of acquisition is the use of foreign nationals working for targeted companies. Many such foreign nationals have been arrested and convicted of stealing corporate intellectual property.

Research and development is expensive. Stealing the secrets of emerging technologies is inherently less expensive. The Internet, the use of third-party vendors, deficient data protection, and a number of other factors increase the ease of illicitly acquiring targeted technologies.

China's goal of dominating technology markets has tough consequences for those investing heavily in research and development. The most valuable targets include an interesting array of intellectual property and trade secrets that will create and fuel the engines of commerce for decades to come.

The Chinese government claims that the first three five-year plans have resulted in a boost of its "overall high-tech development, R&D capacity, socio-economic development, and national security." The government, pleased with 863 Program's success, noted that "in April 2001, the Chinese State Council approved continued implementation of the" 863 Program. The "863 Program continues to play its important role,"[2] the government proclaims, and it is going to be around for a long time. Its mission reflects China's quest for technological superiority gained through the efforts of others, which then translates into economic supremacy. Inadequate security among many companies makes the job easier for China.

The "important role" is, to varying degrees, tantamount to stealing proprietary secrets. China says its tenth five-year plan is intended to help the country "gain a foothold in the world arena," which it clearly has done. The government also states that it intends to "strive to achieve breakthroughs in key technical fields that concern the national economic lifeline and national security."

But China is singularly responsible for the transfer of technology. U.S. companies have helped. U.S. companies were selling advanced encryption technology to that country's military as far back as the late 1990s. Despite the U.S. government's protestations and attempts to discourage the sale of encryption, based on U.S. national security concerns, the sale of advanced encryption continued. It wasn't illegal to sell it, but there's little doubt it was unwise. To illustrate the seriousness of the issue, until 1992 cryptographic products were on the U.S. Munitions List and subject to the Arms Export Control Act.

This is considered by many to be an issue subject to constitutional consideration under the First Amendment, at least insofar as it concerns controlling access to the technology within the United States. While the U.S. government tried to establish restrictions that would prevent the sale of such powerful technology overseas, the rapid proliferation of encryption proved overwhelming, and the United States could not control it. In the late 1990s, the National Security Agency feared that terrorist groups could use encryption. As it turns out, terrorists do use encryption, and so do transnational criminal groups, as well as nation-states. But the globalization of advanced encryption simply became unenforceable. The chief executive of one emerging security company in the late 1990s was often stopped by federal law enforcement officials at the airport when he was on his way to work with the Chinese government and the military. The officers would try to intimidate him, but the tactic did not work.

The U.S. government knew that there were individuals who were willing to face prosecution, that the technology industry was growing dramatically, and that a lot of money was driving the industry. After all, this was at the height of the so-called dot-com era. From 1997 to the first quarter of 2000, there was a technology bubble, with companies valued far beyond what their bottom-line results showed. Basically, the government could not impede the spread of this critical information, and China was a principal beneficiary. In this case, China did not have to steal the technology to protect its own information and to obfuscate its communications and shield them from the rest of the world. It didn't have to. Companies in the United States simply sold it the technology.

China's tactical objective was to "leapfrog" over its competition in the constantly evolving global market. Inside China, Project 863 seen as enhancing its competitive posture. And that perspective is all that matters to China as it pursues global leadership status, selling not only to its own burgeoning population but to countries throughout the world as well.

These series of five-year plans require what the Chinese refer to as "Relevant Measures," a framework for the implementation of such a massive initiative. The measures include a number of basic considerations that illustrate a comprehensive approach to China's "macro-development." Specifically, the measures include:

- Encourage innovation. This is defined as intellectual property development. Of course, innovation is also the illicit acquisition of proprietary information, which reduces the actual requirement of internal innovation in China. This saves China a great deal of R&D investment at a time when its economy is starting to show signs of weakness.
- Enhance the innovation capacity of enterprises.
- Strengthen intellectual property rights. This is in reference to protecting China's internally developed intellectual property. China has become a signatory to the World Trade Organization and is now engaged in global commerce, so its own intellectual property is now at greater risk of compromise by other countries engaged in espionage against it.
- Strengthen the integration of Program 863 with local high-tech development. (See the discussion of North Korean cyber espionage later in this chapter regarding the economically struggling northeastern industrial region of China.) Local high-tech development is often fueled by cyber espionage against specific targets, based on needs analysis. The Chinese government states that "we initiated guidance projects to guide local high-tech development and associated industries to nurture economic growth sources."[3]
- Encourage international economic cooperation. This is a reference to what China refers to as its "Program on Major International Cooperation Projects." It is reasonable for any major economy to cooperate with other nations as a vehicle to create and satisfy market opportunity and demand. However, in the case of China, at least in part, international cooperation is code for gaining access to the technologies of others and then acquiring elements of those technologies in order to better serve the economic interests of China. In other words, it is economic espionage.

While medical and pharmaceutical technologies have long been in the crosshairs of Project 863, other valuable intellectual property and trade secrets are the focus of its unrelenting and highly effective data collection apparatus. Six key technologies have been identified by China as essential to its global competitiveness:

1. Information technology
2. Advanced materials

3. Biotechnology and advanced agricultural technology
4. Advanced manufacturing and automation
5. Energy technology
6. Resource and environment technology

In more detail, these include:

1. Information technology (IT):
   ▪ Computer software and hardware technology
   ▪ Communication technology
   ▪ Information acquisition and processing technology
   ▪ Information security technology

   IT is the building block of the future. There is little doubt that China has used IT to construct the framework for its massive cyber capability, which seems second to none. Of course, using IT aggressively and offensively is easier when one is not constrained from moving boldly and decisively against other nations. Hardware, software, communications technology, and information acquisition and processing technologies are key targets. Look at the impact of IT in the last decade and a half. The workplace—not to mention the home—has been transformed. Desktop computers have often been replaced by laptop computers. Laptop computer sales have slowed because of the emergence of tablets and smartphones. Social media use has grown dramatically. IT not only changes the way people live and work, it creates jobs, powers economies, and enables virtually all elements of the economy.

2. Advanced materials:
   ▪ Photoelectronic materials and devices technology
   ▪ Special functional materials technology
   ▪ High-performance structural materials technology

   Advanced materials are key to energy efficiency. Aerospace and defense industries are critical beneficiaries and especially susceptible to loss. Photoelectronic materials and devices and high-performance structural materials are highly sought after in Project 863.

3. Biotechnology and advanced agricultural technology:
   ▪ Bioengineering technology
   ▪ Gene manipulation technology
   ▪ Bioinformation technology

   Targets include technologies in bioengineering, gene manipulation, and bioinformation that will be used to feed growing populations within and outside of China. This is a contemporary version of capturing hearts and minds: Feed the bodies, and the hearts and minds will follow. It can be expected that China's expansion into Africa will include agricultural technologies.

4. Advanced manufacturing and automation technology:
   ▪ Contemporary integrated manufacturing systems (CIMS)
   ▪ Robotics technologies

   Even in a country of massive labor supply, CIMS, or contemporary integrated manufacturing systems, and robotics are important. China as manufacturer to the world is the theme. This is the path to global competitiveness across many industries, and can be expected to improve not only cost consideration but also quality.

5. Energy technology:
   ▪ Sustainable energy technology
   ▪ Clean coal technology

   Sustainable energy technology and clean coal technology are critical. Energy makes the world go round; it is a vital currency to every economy. Dominate energy, manipulate the world. The implications are enormous. China has also expressed a strong interest in green energy, in both domestic as well as international applications, and is acquiring knowledge of solar and wind energies as well as petroleum.

6. Resource and environment technology:
   ▪ Marine resources exploitation technology
   ▪ Marine biotechnology
   ▪ Ocean monitoring technology
   ▪ Technologies for the prevention of environmental pollution

   Marine resources exploitation, ocean monitoring technologies, and the technology associated with environmental pollution prevention are growth sectors. Emerging nations contribute pollutants as never before. China envisions leadership in cleaning up the planet, even as the air in Beijing clouds the city and its moral authority. China's heavy-industry region in the northeastern part of the country is particularly polluted.

But moral authority isn't the issue upon which the future hinges. Now that China has awakened to the opportunity, shouldn't industry awaken to the threat and take immediate action to protect its assets and value?

China has launched what are called APTs, or advanced persistent threats, against U.S. targets, in addition to acquiring information through academic and industry conferences and utilizing foreign nationals who go to work for U.S. companies.

An APT is exactly what it sounds like. It is technically sophisticated, and it is also continuous. And it is most certainly a threat. The security company Symantec Corporation, a Fortune 500 company, has been analyzing APTs, and one in particular is of concern. Symantec refers to it as Hidden Lynx, a reference to words embedded in the malicious computer code used in the attacks.

According to Symantec, the Chinese cyber attack group is very sophisticated, as well as patient. It is equally voracious in its appetite for information. Symantec believes that "this group is most likely a professional hacker-for-hire operation" that is "contracted by clients to provide information. They steal on demand . . . hence the wide variety and range of targets."[4]

Symantec believes the group is comprised of between 50 and 100 skilled hackers and is "organized into at least two distinctive teams . . . both tasked with carrying out different activities using different tools and techniques." One of the attack teams, Symantec suggests, is an elite group that is deployed to crack the most valuable and hardened targets, and has been carrying out attacks for about three years. Hundreds of organizations have been hit by Hidden Lynx.

Slightly more than half of the assaults have been on U.S. organizations. But there have also been Hidden Lynx attacks against targets in Taiwan, Hong Kong, and even mainland China itself. Other targets were located in Japan, Canada, Germany, Russia, Australia, and South Korea. Key industrial sectors hit by Hidden Lynx include information and communications technologies, aerospace and defense, financial services, energy, even marketing and government. Clearly, as noted by Symantec, this is a diversified list. However, such a distributed range of countries and industries does not necessarily mean that the hackers are working for a variety of clients. This could be the case, but the range of targets may also reflect China's internal interests in capturing data in support of its own developmental and expansionary efforts, which are consistent with Project 863 targets. The fact is, China contracts with hacker groups, transnational cyber crime affiliates, to conduct a variety of attacks against a variety of targets. In either scenario, the threat is real, it is advanced, and it is persistent.

China is believed by many in government and industry to be behind a number of cyber attacks against commercial interests of the nature and range cited by Symantec. Independent research indicates that IP addresses captured in victim companies' logs or electronic records of system activity have been verified as originating in Hong Kong, Guangzhou, and Shenzhen. Tens if not hundreds of millions of electronic records have been compromised as a result of cyber attacks associated with IP addresses registered in those three cities, among others, in China, and elsewhere, including countries associated with a high level of transnational cyber crime.

A CASE OF CYBER ESPIONAGE CONSPIRACY?

The 2013 case of North Korean espionage against South Korea is likely a working example of Project 863 and what may be referred to as the "axis of cyber evil," a realignment of nations embracing on the basis of need.

The end of the Cold War marked the disintegration of the nations of the Soviet bloc, the nations that were subject to the control and direction of the Soviet Union. In the post–Cold War era, those nations sought independence, and some of them have become technologically competent. Unfortunately, some have also become centers of cyber crime and supportive of nation-state espionage. In fact, many cyber breach investigations reveal close linkages between China and Russia as well as other Eastern European countries.

There's an interesting realignment that has taken place. It isn't a Soviet bloc model. That wouldn't work today. But there is a more loosely configured strategy, one that does not require a Soviet-like occupation of aligned states. A Cold War model would be less likely to work today. Whereas the model during the Cold War was driven by politics, this new era of the axis of cyber evil is based on the Internet and is a far more enduring framework, one driven not by dogma but by economics and the lure of growth and power through market dominance. The Internet is an empowering and irresistible aphrodisiac. At its most basic level, it is simple, easy to use, inexpensive, and absorbing. Becoming digital is becoming part of the future. And becoming part of the future requires a lot of information from a lot of sources.

China, Russia, Syria, Iran, and North Korea, long-established cyber threats, are evolving into this post–Cold War axis of cyber evil, which is escalating in intensity and should be taken seriously by any entity, government or private-sector, that possesses valuable proprietary information. The stakes are getting higher.

This realignment or axis of cyber evil provides China the ability to operate with the protective public policy veil of plausible deniability. Assume China wants to acquire a specific technology. Rather than steal it directly over the Internet in a cyber attack, one of its axis of cyber evil partners could do it. This is an important element of China's doctrine, since it is a global economic competitor against the United States, but is also an investor in the U.S. commercial and financial markets. While this dual status of competitor and investor does not in any way diminish China's appetite for valuable U.S. technology, it does make direct and obvious cyber theft against U.S. targets somewhat more sensitive. With the U.S. government continuously challenging China diplomatically for targeting U.S. proprietary interests in this economic cyber war, China is increasingly likely to work through its partners in the axis of cyber evil.

For an industry requiring clean rooms for manufacturing, cyber theft is a dirty business. Often it is difficult to determine exactly who did what, who attacked whom. But in the arena of public perception—and reality—China clearly stands out. Unless some cyber warfare counterintelligence group at the National Security Agency knows otherwise and is keeping it secret, the United States doesn't fully understand the absolute cyber capability of China. It works both ways, too; China probably does not fully understand U.S. cyber capabilities. After the defection of former NSA systems administrator Edward Snowden, China and Russia know a lot more, but there is also a lot neither nation knows.

Is it possible that Snowden's disclosures will embolden China? Perhaps. From China's point of view, such classified data should be protected at all costs. Yet Snowden was able to access tremendous volumes of data. Coworkers saw him do so but never said anything because he was a systems administrator, certainly not a senior-level position, but one with great access, and one that should have been more tightly monitored. Those issues are cited openly in the press, and China has no doubt been watching with great interest.

Given China's success in stealing U.S. information, and given the bumbling errors committed in the classified defense community, China will almost certainly escalate its quest for more information, believing such pursuits to be relatively low-risk and carrying relatively inconsequential penalties. From China's perspective, given the risk-reward calculus, there seems to be little incentive not to pursue information acquisition.

There is another downside. When other countries are witness to the level of cyber theft from U.S. targets, it signals vulnerabilities and makes a statement about the will of the United States to defend itself against cyber attack. While China can demand that its industries practice strong security, such demands in the United States and many other countries are not possible, other than regulatory requirements. And regulatory compliance by companies is overall quite low. In capitalist systems, companies need to see the financial value in protecting information. That level of clarity is sorely lacking, especially, though not exclusively, in unregulated markets.

It comes down to this: If China wants to continue its diplomatic and commercial business with the United States, it makes more sense for it to in effect outsource some of its cyber espionage to its participating axis of cyber evil nations, which need the infusion of Chinese capital. This does not necessarily mean that China will reduce its direct cyber assaults. But it does suggest that plausible deniability will enable China's expansionary quest in support of more proprietary information collection.

Think about it this way: The origination point or epicenter of an attack is not always immediately obvious, at least not initially. It is technically feasible to do what is known as redirect an attack. Suppose that China wants to launch an attack to acquire restricted information from the United States. In one actual case, in an attempt to sneak into U.S. cyber space, it launched an attack but routed it through a U.S. university. The goal was to trick people working in the defense industry and the military to click on a link, which would then download into the user's computer a malicious software program that would enable China to capture any keystrokes made by the user, such as passwords that would then give greater access into computer systems.

By rerouting or redirecting a cyber attack, China can make the claim of plausible deniability, allowing it more time in which to deny the attack and divert investigative efforts directed against the attacker. This is why plausible deniability is important, and it is also why the alignment of nations forming an axis of cyber evil is important to the strategic interests of China. Also, given the U.S. and international sanctions levied against Iran and North Korea, for example, additional economic sanctions for engaging in cyber attacks against the United States are minimally threatening. However, this raises the specter of how the United States may respond to a cyber attack by one of the countries mentioned. Already, Iran and the United States have tangled in the cyber arena, and this can be expected to continue, if not escalate, as tensions heighten in the Middle East.

Look for China and Russia to more actively engage the axis of cyber evil for technology and economic espionage, cyber disinformation, cyber disruption, and cyber confusion in the marketplace. Each of these kinds of cyber attacks creates uncertainly and has the capability to instill a loss of confidence, perhaps in a company's stock price. Such attacks can also serve as distractions to shield cyber espionage. The fact is, these nations are expert at using the Internet, and they have strong experience in attack strategy and in yielding results.

One reason the axis of cyber evil may be an appealing strategy in support of Project 863 is that China already denies that it launches cyber attacks against the United States, and it wants to be able to continue to do so. Attacks coming from Iran, Syria, North Korea, or elsewhere against U.S. interests make the perfect cover for China because of the poor state of relations between these nations and the United States. That these foreign powers would launch aggressive attacks against U.S. interests is easily understandable, even predictable.

Every company in every country engaged in some form of electronic commerce—which is virtually every enterprise in every developing or developed nation—should be alert to any cyber attack. Every CEO, every member of the audit and risk committee of the board of directors, every executive with fiduciary responsibility needs to know about this risk to the enterprise. Unfortunately, far too few are aware of it.

Consider the Syrian Electronic Army, or SEA, thought by many to be funded by the Bashar Hafez al-Assad regime. Until recently, the media and diplomatic focus on Syria has been on the deployment of deadly chemical weapons against its own people. But now we are witness to cyber attacks on the institutions that have been critical of Assad and Syria: the *New York Times*, the BBC, the Qatari government, National Public Radio, even Al Jazeera. The attacks have caused various levels of cyber disruption, and are believed to have begun with very sophisticated phishing attacks.

Iran has been engaged in attacking U.S. bank web sites for more than a year, creating operational disruption in the form of denial-of-service attacks while demonstrating that U.S. targets are not by any measure immune.

China's cyber attacks are well known, despite its diplomatic protestations. Transnational organized crime is equally well established. But North Korea's recent attacks against South Korean targets are particularly interesting, because North Korea is an element of the axis of cyber evil.

The attacks, recently made public by antimalware company Kaspersky Lab, are of concern for two reasons: first, because of the selection of attack targets, and second, because of North Korea's relationship with China. The targets included the Sejong Institute, a South Korea think tank specializing in national security strategy and Korean reunification. This seems to be a clear case of political espionage. The Korea Institute for Defense Analyses is a national security and defense quasi-governmental organization, so it too is an understandable target for North Korea, as is the South Korean Ministry of Unification. One of the more intriguing espionage targets was South Korea's Hyundai Merchant Marine Co. Ltd., part of the Hyundai Group, a diversified corporation.

While the other targets are logical, given North Korean unification and national security concerns, the Hyundai information theft may not be as immediately understandable. It is true that North Korea maintains a merchant marine operation, yet it seems unlikely that this rogue nation-state would benefit substantially and directly from cyber espionage against Hyundai Merchant Marine. South Korea ranks number eight in the global merchant marine market sector, with 1,144 vessels. North Korea, which ranks 34th in the world, maintains a fleet of only 150 vessels, many of which are said not to be seaworthy and reportedly do not stray far from their home ports. (To put this in perspective, Greece is ranked number one, with 3,768 vessels.) It seems improbable that North Korea would steal information for its own competitive positioning, given its anemic economy, deficient fleet operational status, and its maritime scrutiny by many law-abiding nations. The South Korea shipping and global logistics industry possess critical information regarding environmentally clean transport, which is crucial to competitive positioning. In addition, it possesses important trade secrets regarding advanced materials and design.

What is more likely is that either (1) North Korea was hired by China to breach South Korean interests, perhaps the political components of the breach providing strategic cover; (2) North Korea, acting independently, believed that it could sell the information to China; or (3) China launched the attack against South Korea but made it look like the attack was originated by North Korea.

Geography played a part in the cyber attack against South Korea. Ten of the IP address ranges, according to Kaspersky, originated in the Jilin Province network and the Liaoning Province network. Situated in the northeastern region of China, Jilin and Liaoning are near the North Korean and Russian borders. The Internet service providers that serve the region are believed to maintain communication lines into parts of North Korea.

Once a center of heavy industry, with strong Russian, Chinese, and North Korean influence, this region of China has in recent years not fared well economically, and its population exceeds 100 million. Industry sectors include steel, automotive, shipbuilding, aircraft, petroleum, and manufacturing. There are about a dozen key universities in the region, many of them with strong science and technology programs.

And here is the point: China has an aggressive revitalization plan that was developed by its National Development and Reform Commission (NDRC). The NDRC economic development report, translated from Chinese, states that "China's participation in international competition, the use of domestic and foreign resources and markets to accelerate the pace of expansion of trade . . . to create more opportunities" is part of its strategy. The report also states that "economic development is not sufficient."

However, there is a more direct link that suggests China is the beneficiary of the Hyundai information. Citing that its "high tech industries [are] inadequate," the report documents the need for China to significantly improve its "international level of shipbuilding" and "accelerate the development of [its] high-tech industry." Perhaps most indicative of China's involvement is its stated objective to pursue, as part of its regional economic strategy, an upgrade of its "logistics management, logistics and distribution facilities," and its "integrated logistics system in Northeast China." Of course, global integrated logistics is the business of Hyundai Merchant Marine.

Regardless of specifics—and we may never know exactly what occurred— it is obvious that North Korea has global reach. It is also obvious that it has an important relationship with China. Given China's voracious appetite for an extraordinary range of information that it will use to fuel its global economic leadership, companies possessing intellectual property and trade secrets are at extreme risk. And because most proprietary information is unregulated and is therefore not subject to basic protections, the risk of compromise is heightened.

This is not a call to regulate proprietary information. But every audit and risk committee member of the board of directors, every CEO and general counsel should ask questions about the entity's ability to protect the information that is anticipated to contribute to current and future corporate revenue streams and enhance value. This is not just a security problem. It is an issue of critical corporate governance, clarity of mission, and long-term reputation and market competitiveness. It is, equally, a national economic security imperative.

The Internet has both complicated and simplified technology espionage. It has simplified spying by making it easier to steal secrets through cyber attacks. A tremendous amount of sensitive information is undersecured or, in many instances, is not secured at all. Some cases clearly illustrate the lack of security, which led to breaches.

In one case, a company managing another company's sensitive regulated data had no antivirus software in place. Two variants of a cyber attack easily breached the firm's information system. Upon forensic examination, two specific Internet protocol (IP) types were identified in the system, both originating in China, and others from Eastern Europe. There were authorized IP addresses, and then there were unauthorized IP addresses, which were the attack vehicles. These unauthorized or toxic IP addresses were the true threat. But they can be hard to distinguish from authorized IP addresses.

The majority were from China. The authorized IP address is a label that gets assigned to each computing device attached to the Internet. Knowing that address enables tracking (there are exceptions). In the case referenced, the breached company had an IP address in its computer environment that was unauthorized; it was not supposed to be there. That unauthorized IP address basically served as a communications beacon, broadcasting from inside the company's network. There was no antivirus software in place, so the unauthorized IP address was able to identify sensitive information and communicate that information back to China.

But there was another type of IP address in the company's computer environment, and here's what makes the predicament more complicated. This type of IP address was actually authorized to be in the client environment. However, because there was no software that could identify the IP address as risky, these IP addresses too were broadcasting protected, regulated data back to China. This second type of IP address was authorized because it was actually transmitted to the company by its corporate customer.

When this condition occurs—an IP address belonging to a customer is toxic—there is often great reticence by the breached company to bring this to the attention of its corporate customer for fear of alienating that customer. But the fact is that a customer's toxic IP address is no less malicious than any other type of malicious IP address. Hesitation, or even refusal, to alert the customer to the presence of that toxic IP address likely elevates that customer's risk as well. In effect, no one wants to tell the emperor that he is dressed in a toxic IP address. This allows the breach to occur.

Eventually, though, the customer is likely to discover the toxic IP address in any case. That can happen in several ways. The customer may itself be subject to data theft. Or if customer data is breached while at the company managing its data, the service provider may have to notify the company that its data was breached, perhaps by IP addresses in its own network.

Though the Internet has in many ways simplified information management, there's the complexity of it to deal with. The complexity in the equation comes with protecting restricted information. The Internet makes it easier to illicitly acquire information. In principle this sounds straightforward, even obvious. Yet many companies—somewhat unbelievably—do not seem to accept that the threat is real and that the risk is critical to their value proposition. Some executives do not accept that their company is likely to be targeted by transnational criminal networks or by nation-states engaged in espionage. Many small and medium-size companies assume that they are simply not on anyone's cyber attack radar. "No one knows who we are, we're too small," they say. They seem to think they are invisible, and therefore invulnerable to cyber attack and cyber espionage. This is not the case now. Maybe at one time it was, but not anymore. It's a new world.

They are not invisible. Social media, third-party vendors, mobile devices, e-mail, and the Web all have made sure that invisibility is a condition of the past. The Web and the Internet have proven to be the great democratizers of competitive presence. A one-person enterprise has the capability today to incite, incent, invite, and inspire global markets, largely without the traditional boundaries and restraints of a generation ago, or even a decade ago, before the wildfire of social media.

While many nations conduct cyber espionage against the United States and its economic allies, there is no doubt that China reigns supreme among them. Twenty-first-century China has tremendous cyber capabilities. History, timing, culture, the economy, changes in industry, global competition, sheer will, plausible deniability, deception, denials, and technology have coalesced to place China at the forefront of proprietary information theft. Its capabilities seem unmatched. China seems to see the theft of intellectual property in pursuit of its own economic security as a form of its own manifest destiny. Perhaps what Americans in the nineteen century saw as westward expansion and the building of a new nation, China envisions as its own emergence into a highly competitive landscape, one dominated by a number of technologies critical to sustainable competitive positioning.

Some years ago a company wanted to test the quality of its third-party data management vendors. The company possessed a significant number of trade secrets, which made up a significant amount of its current and future financial value. Cyber attacks against its vendors in three countries were authorized. After several weeks of effort, the company was presented with the cyber attack study results. A data management vendor in Europe had been easily pene-trated, as had one in the United States. The one data center that was virtually impenetrable, locked down securely, was in China, managed by China Telecom Corporation Limited, which is owned by the state and maintains subsidiary operations in 31 Chinese provinces.

There is another disturbing development in cyber espionage. A form of hacking, it is more insidious than a team of hackers in a foreign nation stealing proprietary corporate or government information. The reason it is more insidious is that the victim is actually purchasing hardware and software that broadcasts data out of the purchasing organization's information and communications system. The threat is in the global telecommunications supply chain. This has become a serious controversy between the United States and

China. While China denies that its companies are spying on the United States, either through traditional cyber attack methods or through the same of hardware and software configured to capture information and send it back to China, the United States believes otherwise.

In late 2012, the House Permanent Select Committee on Intelligence issued its findings on China's telecommunications spying in a report called "Investigative Report on the U.S. National Security Issues Posed by Chinese Telecommunications Companies Huawei and ZTE."[5] The report is damning. The investigation, which focused on China's top two telecommunications manufacturers., was a supply chain risk assessment consisting of two principal parts. The first part was basically a discovery and analysis program. The goal was to evaluate the companies on the basis of open-source materials in order to assess their corporate histories, operations, financial information, and ties to the Chinese government and the Chinese Communist Party. The second part of the study looked at the capability of the U.S. intelligence community in "appropriately prioritizing and resourcing for supply chain risk evaluation."

Despite the level of effort expended by the Select Committee, it concluded that neither company was cooperative. The committee claimed that the companies failed to provide sufficient evidence to satisfy its concerns about electronic spying. Disappointed in the level of cooperation from both Chinese telecommunications firms, the Select Committee determined that "neither company provided specific details about the precise role of each company's Chinese Communist Party Committee. Furthermore, neither company provided detailed information about its operations in the United States."

But Huawei in particular "failed to provide thorough information about its corporate structure, history, ownership, operations, financial arrangements, or management. Most importantly, neither company provided sufficient internal documentation or other evidence to support the limited answers they did provide to Committee investigators." The Select Committee did receive information from both current and previous Huawei employees and industry experts suggesting that the company was violating U.S. laws and international standards of business behavior.

There is apparent disagreement about how Huawei USA actually operates within the United States. With its U.S. headquarters in Plano, Texas, established in 2005, the company maintains that the "parent company does not require approval for individual contracts in the United States," according to the report, signaling that Huawei operates independently in the United States. It did admit that the board of directors in China sets the general business operational guidelines. But there is no consensus on this subject relative to who actually sets the specific operational guidelines and who signs contracts. The Select Committee interviewed several former Huawei employees who told a significantly different version of the story. A number of sources told the Select Committee that business decisions require approval directly from China. Senior-level executives in the United States, according to an individual with firsthand knowledge, are not allowed to sign cyber security contracts in the United States without approval from China. In one case, according to testimony, such a contract signed by a Huawei USA executive was "repudiated," or overturned, in China.

According to the report, "The investigation concludes that the risks associated with Huawei's and ZTE's provision of equipment to U.S. critical infrastructure could undermine core U.S. national-security interests."

Under questioning by Congress, ZTE officials were very circumspect and were not forthcoming with regard to whether or not members of the Chinese government, military, or Communist Party were involved with ZTE and served on the board. For a time, ZTE refused to answer questions. It did, however, at a later date provide some information that is of concern.

A number of members of the Communist Party serve within ZTE, and two of these representatives appear to serve on the board of directors, where they would wield considerable influence. The concern is that the two board members may have a conflict of interest in their duties to the Communist Party and to ZTE shareholders. Independent ZTE director Timothy Steinert told the Select Committee that "in my experience and to my knowledge, no member of ZTE's Board of Directors has raised for consideration an interest on behalf of the Chinese Government, the People's Liberation Army or the Chinese Communist Party."

This assertion, though, failed to allay concerns of Congress. "Since at least two members of the Board are also members of the Chinese State Party," stated the Select Committee, "it is impossible to know whether the votes of the Board are conducted without influence by the Chinese Communist Party."

The Select Committee was concerned enough about the inadequacy of the cooperation of the two companies that it issued an advisory to government agencies and to private industry as well. Use extreme caution, the committee advised. In general, the committee has stated that the United States should be suspicious of Chinese companies further penetrating the domestic telecommunications market.

It recommends that the intelligence community keep its private-sector classified contractors informed on the threat of the Chinese telecommunications companies. Given the threat to U.S. national security interests, the Select

Committee wants the Committee on Foreign Investment in the United States (CFIUS) to make sure that neither Huawei nor ZTE be allowed to take over, acquire, or merge with any U.S. telecommunications company. In fact, the Select Committee has recommended legislative proposals that would expand the authority of CFIUS to include purchasing agreements.

No Huawei or ZTE equipment, or even component parts, should be used in any U.S. government systems, and especially not in any sensitive systems. Private-sector contractors working with the U.S. government are also discouraged from using equipment from these Chinese companies. But the Select Committee didn't stop there. It "strongly encourages" private-sector companies to consider the long-term security risks of doing business with either Huawei or ZTE.

The Select Committee concluded that "based on available classified and unclassified information, Huawei and ZTE cannot be trusted to be free of foreign state influence and thus pose a security threat to the United States and to our systems." Additionally, the committee wants to see Congress and enforcement offices in the executive branch investigate unfair trade practices by the Chinese telecommunications sector, with specific attention to the continuing financial support for companies like Huawei and ZTE.

In fact, Congress concluded in its study that ZTE failed to provide any answers about its compliance with U.S. intellectual property laws and export control restrictions. Nor did the company provide any information about its infrastructure projects in the United States. It also failed to answer questions "that would explain whether ZTE purposely bids on projects below cost and how the company is able to sustain these losses." The implication, of course, is that ZTE is buying U.S. business at a loss in order to be able to install its equipment in U.S. infrastructure for the purpose of acquiring proprietary information and reporting it to Chinese government authorities as part of a technology and economic espionage program.

Under questioning by Congress, ZTE did make some interesting comments, which provide insight into the company's, and China's, intent. ZTE, which employs approximately 300 people in five U.S. research and development centers, stated that basically it was here to help the United States by assisting in what it referred to as rural infrastructure and broadband communications needs. ZTE was engaged in public service. However, company officials finally admitted that there was nothing charitable in the ZTE presence. They even admitted that the intent of ZTE was to get a "foothold" in the United States and increase their knowledge of U.S. technology. ZTE stated that it was willing to provide equipment below cost in order to better understand the market. Naturally, that information is funneled back to the Chinese government.

ACCORDING TO THE SELECT COMMITTEE . . .

Interestingly, it is being recommended by the Select Committee that one way for Chinese companies to become more open is to have them listed "on a western stock exchange with advanced transparency requirements, offering more consistent review by independent third-party evaluators of their financial information and cyber-security processes." This would also result in "complying with U.S. legal standards of information and evidentiary production, and obeying all intellectual-property laws and standards." Huawei in particular, the Select Committee says, "must become more transparent and responsive to U.S. legal obligations."

China continues to deny all allegations of impropriety, a position it has been adopting for decades.

U.S. government systems, particularly systems containing sensitive and restricted information, should not include Huawei or ZTE equipment, including component parts. Similarly, government contractors, particularly those working on contracts for sensitive U.S. programs, should exclude ZTE or Huawei equipment from their systems. This is a simple precaution, but it is leading to delicate conversations between the two governments, with considerable economic and diplomatic impact.

The Select Committee extended its warning to the private sector in the United States, noting that the long-term security risks of doing business with Chinese companies are considerable. "U.S. network providers and systems developers are strongly encouraged to seek other vendors for their projects," according to the report. In its closing recommendation, the Select Committee made it clear that Congress needs to consider legislation that more adequately addresses "the risk posed by telecommunications companies with nation-state ties or otherwise not clearly trusted to build critical infrastructure. Such legislation could include increasing information sharing among private sector entities, and an expanded role for the CFIUS process to include purchasing agreements."

China and the United States are at odds. China steals U.S. information and the United States has sold encryption to the Chinese military. China is the third largest export market for U.S. goods. The United States is China's single largest export market. The United States and China have announced measures to strengthen macroeconomic cooperation, promote open trade, enhance global cooperation and international rules, and foster financial stability and reform.

The word from the U.S. Department of State is that "China and the U.S. work closely with the international community to address threats to global security, including North Korea and Iran's nuclear programs." But the problem is far more complex. While it may reasonably be argued that China, given its surface level of cooperation with the United States, as well as its significant financial investment in the United States and in other Western economies, would be an unlikely participant in a massive military cyber strike against the United States, China should never be underestimated. It is clear that China ultimately wants to dominate the global economy. The country will continue to steal commercial and government information until such time as defenses are adequate to the task of defeating China's cyber attacks. And China will not launch a major disruptive cyber strike against U.S. interests until such time as it may serve a strategic purpose to do so. When that happens, the task will likely be outsourced to an axis of cyber evil country, providing China with its great wall of plausible deniability.

Much will be written in the coming months and years about China's economic espionage and the charges that have been filed by the U.S. Department of Justice. A grand jury in the Western District of Pennsylvania indicted five members of the Chinese military on charges that included economic espionage and computer hacking. It is too soon to determine how serious the U.S. government is about pressing China on the issue, but this much is clear: China will never allow its military to stand trial in the United States. A number of strategies are available to the United States to make economic espionage against it costly to China. Whatever strategy adopted by the United States, there must be an appetite to play hardball. And that willingness remains unclear at this point.

Said Benjamin Dubuc, who formerly taught English in China after graduating from college, "While accessing my GMail account . . . [some] e-mails would never be sent/received, others would periodically disappear from my inbox. Cyber theft entails every station of an assembly line, every ingredient of prescription medicine, every line of a novel, every minute of your favorite movie." China will not ease up voluntarily. It has too much at stake, and U.S. vulnerability is high. So whose undoing will this be?

 NOTES

1. State High-Tech Research and Development Plan, People's Republic of China, www.most.gov.cn/eng/programmes1.

2. Ibid.

3. Ibid.

4. Symantec, "Hidden Lynx—Professional Hackers for Hire," September 17, 2013, www.symantec.com/connect/blogs/hidden-lynx-professional-hackers-hire.

5. House Permanent Select Committee on Intelligence, "Investigative Report on the U.S. National Security Issues Posed by Chinese Telecommunications Companies Huawei and ZTE," October 8, 2012, https://intelligence.house .gov/sites/intelligence.house.gov/files/documents/Huawei-ZTE%20Investiga tive%20Report%20%28FINAL%29.pdf.

CHAPTER THREE

Cyber Al Qaeda Poses a Threat to Critical Infrastructure

It is very important to concentrate on hitting the U.S. economy through all means possible.

—*Osama bin Laden*

TERRORISTS POSSESS seven basic weapons. These include biological weapons, chemical weapons, nuclear explosive devices, radiological dispersion, small-arms attacks such as the one deployed in Kenya at Westgate Mall in September 2013, propaganda, and cyber attacks. They have demonstrated the capability to hijack airplanes, kidnap executives and members of the government, and bring terror to civilian populations. Cyber attacks are somewhat unique in that they are also a force multiplier, in addition to being a direct threat through the interruption of communications, command, and control.

Like other kinds of terrorist threats, a cyber attack can result in various levels of destruction, including death. Now or in the future, will terrorists have the capability to interfere with commercial and general aviation? Will they be able to disable large areas of the electrical grid? What would happen in the event that emergency and medical services were interrupted?

While this may be unlikely to result in a worst-case scenario today, what about tomorrow?

Is the threat of the cyber terrorist overblown? Many believe that it is. Among them are influential people in government and industry. Not to believe in cyber terrorism is not popular. A lot of money, in government and industry, is being invested in defending against the threat of cyber terror. It's big business. Others believe that the threat is uncomfortably real, that critical infrastructure is very vulnerable to various types of cyber attack, and that such an attack is coming. To be fair, it would be dangerous not to prepare for a cyber terror attack. After all, Osama bin Laden was a laptop user, as are many members of Al Qaeda. Many of them now use smartphones and tablets. But the larger threat is that an entire generation of terrorists is cyber literate, is motivated to attack, and believes strongly that such attacks are not only justified but mandatory. Not to prepare for such an attack would be negligent.

Is there a real cyber threat from terrorists? The answer is yes, absolutely.

But here are a few considerations. Yes, there are serious vulnerabilities in critical infrastructure. This is addressed in Presidential Policy Directive (PPD) 21, signed in February 2013. PPD-21 defines critical infrastructure this way: "The Nation's critical infrastructure provides the essential services that underpin American society. Proactive and coordinated efforts are necessary to strengthen and maintain secure, functioning, and resilient critical infra-structure—including assets, networks, and systems—that are vital to public confidence and the Nation's safety, prosperity, and well-being."[1] This gets to the point of why it is important to protect it. "It is the policy of the United States to strengthen the security and resilience of its critical infrastructure against both physical and cyber threats," according to the directive.

Al Qaeda and various affiliated groups influenced by it do pose a threat to critical infrastructure. But that threat is not necessarily an electronic Pearl Harbor planned and executed by terrorist groups. No one can say for sure what the actual plan is for attacking the United States, unless the intelligence agencies possess such information, in which case it would be classified. What is known is that attacks will occur, many of them, but there is an argument to be made that the Internet is a vital tool in the terrorist arsenal—a tool terrorists don't want to do without. Terrorists use the Internet much like any other group. They utilize it to recruit other terrorists to join their cause. They use the Internet to transfer money, to launder money, to raise operating capital, to plan strategy and attacks. They use the Internet to create confusion through the distribution of disinformation, to hack into other systems, and to both develop and deliver computer viruses. Sometimes they are allied with nation-states to commit a variety of crimes.

The Internet is a tool. Tools are not goals; tools are things that help build or destroy. Tools are valuable, and are not disposable. Before a terrorist group launches a massive, disabling cyber attack against critical infrastructure, it needs to consider the consequences of its actions. Will it cause its funding to dry up? Will it result in a drop in recruitment? Will it lose the ability to communicate with its cells operating throughout the range of critical infrastructure? Will it result in confusion for the terrorists?

There are lots of terrorist organizations with many agendas, many blending in with society, a generation of terrorists who are likely holding down professional jobs, balancing careers and jihad, unlike many, but not all, of those who came before them. But it does bring into question the wisdom, from the terrorist perspective, of the value in shutting down, or trying to shut down, the very intricately connected systems that in part fuel jihadist ambition.

 ## A DISABLED AMERICA

There have long been concerns about attacks upon the systems that run America, chief among them the electrical grid. A disabled America would be a prize that would cheer even the most dour of terrorists. But disabled how? Disabled to prevent critical infrastructure operations? Or disabled to inconvenience? For years, the country has been in cyber evolution—e-mail, the information superhighway, the World Wide Web, electronic commerce, and then portability, first in the form of laptop computers, followed by smartphones and tablets and innumerable applications, plus the explosion of social media. There are smart homes, featuring the ability to set the temperature of any room, lock any electronically activated door in the house from anywhere in the world. And then there are electronically activated industrial controls—access values, gates, dams, various Internet-enabled switches that are part of the electrical grid. In an Internet-enabled world, there is always the chance for an Internet-disabled result.

The goal of the terrorist is to inspire fear. There's no doubt that crippling the electrical grid would go a long way toward creating fear. Electricity runs most everything; not having it generates fear.

Can we expect an Al Qaeda or other terrorist entity strike at U.S. critical infrastructure? That's a near certainty. They want to create confusion, disrupt the global supply chain, interfere with the strategy and operations of capitalism at work, and create uncertainty about financial services, food, water, health services, law and order, and the other elements necessary to sustain a functioning society. But their targets are more likely to be focused. Historically terrorists have not been known to be expert hackers. But they can buy that capability and, increasingly, recruit it. The historic status quo is changing. They may target the Internet-enabled controls for dams or a water supply, a power-generating station, even a hospital. It is unlikely they are under the delusion that they can cast the entire nation into darkness by launching a massive cyber attack against the electrical grid.

While the idea of a disabled Internet, death to America, and capitalism held hostage at the hands of terrorists no doubt gives rise to inspirational messaging, the cold reality is that the Internet is essential to Al Qaeda's recruitment and conversion programming. The Internet is an important component of Al Qaeda's revenue generation, which is linked to narcotics trafficking, which is in turn linked to organized crime and money laundering. This is one reason that what has become known as a potential digital Pearl Harbor is more likely a goal of North Korea or Iran, not Al Qaeda or a subordinate affiliate.

Inspire magazine is an online English-language magazine that is believed to be published by Al Qaeda and is used to promote the cause of global jihad. It is used to recruit terrorists, to raise capital for terrorist attacks, and for other purposes. *Inspire* without the Internet will have the reach of homing pigeons— not unimportant, but extremely limited. It is doubtful that *Inspire* would survive the absence of the Internet, probably an unacceptable proposition to the terrorist recruitment effort.

"It used to take an entire nation to wage war," observe Winn Schwartau in his 2002 novel *Pearl Harbor Dot Com*. "Today it takes only one man." Mr. Schwartau is best known for having coined the phrase "electronic Pearl Harbor" and is known as the civilian architect of information warfare.

More than 20 years ago he was asked to report to Congress on the state of cyber readiness in the private sector. In reporting to the Subcommittee on Technology and Competiveness, he testified that "government and commercial computer systems are so poorly protected today they can essentially be considered defenseless—an Electronic Pearl Harbor waiting to happen." He then, prophetically, addressed the issue of privacy: "As a result of inadequate security planning on the part of both the government and the private sector, the privacy of most Americans has virtually disappeared."[2] Move forward more than two decades and things certainly have not gotten any better. But the measure of the loss of privacy is only one metric. The rise of electronic terrorism is arguably even more dangerous.

In the months leading up to September 11, 2001, many in national security knew that something wasn't right. There were even a few within the FBI who knew that the nation was at risk for a major terrorist attack. The signs were there, at least if you looked in the right places. One of the right places to look was on the Internet. The level of Internet chatter by certain groups was escalating. "Chatter," of course, is a form of signals intelligence, or SIGINT. It is measurable. Electronic chatter rises and falls. While it isn't a blueprint of what is going to happen, it is an indicator that something is up. So, yes, there were clues about an attack. Some even knew that the attacks on the United States were imminent. But these were indicators of attack, early warning symptoms.

Electronic chatter today is even more prevalent and an invaluable intelligence and investigative asset. This is likely attributable to several factors. First, even though the formal group known as Al Qaeda may have been downgraded because of the killing of many of its leaders, make no mistake that it is attracting many adherents from a number of emerging and developed countries. What the formal terrorist organization may lack in actual numbers of soldiers, it more than makes up for in its ability to inspire legions of others who will carry out its objectives around the world. Second, there is more or less unlimited and uninterrupted Internet access, a lot more social media sites for sharing information, and the continuously expanding use of mobile devices, including tablets and smartphones. Third, there is an unending flow of constantly changing information on the Web, a vast source of new intelligence, but also of disinformation. This combination of conditions has laid the foundation for a lot more electronic chatter than in the weeks and months leading up to 9/11. A terrorist group with flexible financial resources has a world stage upon which to act out its ambitions and advertise its agenda, and it seems to be learning how to use that platform in new and creative ways.

The Internet is a vital terrorist tool used in shaping public policy. In fact, it is safe to say that Al Qaeda loves the Internet. To Al Qaeda, which is often underfinanced (the attacks of 9/11 are said to have cost only half a million dollars), highly distributed in numerous countries around the world, the Internet is a tool of extreme usefulness. But the Internet is more than a useful tool. It has become the foundation of Al Qaeda's outreach program. It centers on *Inspire* magazine. Radical Islam has, ironically, embraced the Internet.

As Al Qaeda evolves, it will rely increasingly on *Inspire* to bring in new recruits, to reach a new generation. The social and cultural adoption of tablets and smartphones and social media will significantly contribute to its sphere of influence. And there is another trend that dovetails comfortably with the propaganda and technology trends: that of the new terrorist profile.

Inspire, first published in July 2010, has become an important public relations vehicle, and not only in the Arabian Peninsula where it is believed to be based. It has become a very popular publication. A 2010 issue links the publication to the Boston Marathon bombing. That issue showed jihadists how to build a pressure cooker bomb, the type used in the bombing, and it provided a justification for lashing out at non-Muslims. It is also believed to have influenced the planned bombing of the London Stock Exchange in 2012. It has helped shape terrorist tactics, encouraging Al Qaeda adherents to engage infidels in a variety of ways. With many of Al Qaeda's leaders dead, *Inspire* was a unique opportunity to keep their ideals not only alive but a way to reach budding terrorists around the world, in many countries and cultures.

It is too early to know the extent of the conspiracy involved in the bombing. No doubt some of the investigative findings will remain classified. But this much is clear: Two terrorists, who lived largely beneath the radar, were clearly extremist, and were clearly capable. They executed the plan with near precision. They were also unreservedly inspired. Thanks to *Inspire*, their deadly actions will be used to introduce a new age of terrorist engagement. *Inspire* will use the events associated with the bombings to further its extremist goals, that much is certain.

 ## A NEW AGE: INSPIRING TERRORISTS AND TERRORISM

The goal of *Inspire* is to capitalize on the threat of terror by perpetuating it, aggrandizing it, and praising it as an act of faith above the faith of all others. The result is predictable. Whether before a terrorist attack occurs or in its bloody aftermath, the human and digital imprimatur of *Inspire* is present. Here's how it is may unfold, although perhaps not with the bang of a digital Pearl Harbor.

On the heels of the 2013 Boston Marathon bombing, Chiheb Esseghaier, 30, and Raed Jaser, 35, have been accused in Canada of "conspiring to murder persons unknown . . . in association with a terrorist group" by plotting to attack a passenger train operating between Toronto and New York City. The terrorist group referenced is Al Qaeda. While it remains unclear what the investigation of the Boston bombing will ultimately reveal, the planned assault in Canada is quite clear.

Make no mistake, Al Qaeda may be dazed and in some ways diminished, and perhaps even underfinanced from time to time, but it is far from being dead. Whatever Al Qaeda may have reportedly lost in profound direct frontal assault capability, it has made up for in creativity, stealth, resiliency, and Internet enablement. It would be a mistake, and a misrepresentation, to interpret Al Qaeda's simmering low-intensity presence to be a sign of diminished capacity. In some corners, Al Qaeda's current profile seems to have imbued in the United States and elsewhere a dangerous false sense of security.

Al Qaeda's evolving profile may not be the reincarnation of its 9/11 body, but its spirit remains unchanged and unchecked. The organization that brought us the most infamous day in recent decades is as much a threat today as it ever was. It is just a different threat, as the conspiracy in Canada illustrates.

While the details of the Esseghaier and Jaser case continue to emerge, one thing is clear. Esseghaier led two lives. Pursuing his doctorate in Canada in the field of optical and electrochemical biosensors, he published work on methods of detecting prostate cancer and HIV, among other diseases. Science was the way he earned a paycheck. Jihad seems to be how he defined his life's mission. He isn't the only one.

If there is a new face of terrorism, it may look more like the Boston bombing or the terrorist plan in Canada. While deadly in design and execution, these types of attack lack the sophistication of a 9/11 event, yet such attacks have proven fatal, disruptive, and inspirational to other terrorists. The attackers are skilled computer users.

Such terrorists are said to have engaged in behaviors that showed their disdain for the Canadian government and the country's culture. Esseghaier, it is reported, ripped down a poster of a woman, which he considered to be an affront to Islam. He also chastised a Muslim coworker for paying taxes to the government. Such actions eventually came to the attention of law enforcement and intelligence authorities.

Perhaps the day of the full-time, dedicated jihadist is waning, but jihad is growing in another, perhaps even more dangerous way. Terrorists who lead seemingly double lives are often harder to detect and monitor. Terrorist organizations' financial accounts are monitored more carefully now than on September 10, 2001. Today's terrorists are more likely to have their own checking accounts and an income, making it more complicated to track terrorist financing. Consequently, they may not need as much formal financial support in planning and carrying out attacks. That they are dispersed to target nations and engaged in professional pursuits presents new challenges for the intelligence community, elevating the threat of cyber and physical attacks.

As described in my book *Threat! Managing Risk in a Hostile World*,[3] Kafeel Ahmed, one of the terrorists behind the June 30, 2007, Glasgow International Airport attack, led a double life. He was pursuing a doctorate in fluid dynamics and worked below the radar as an aerospace engineer at an overseas company under contract with Boeing Aerospace and Airbus Industries. But Ahmed is best known for loading his Jeep Cherokee with extra tanks of gasoline and driving it, with accomplice Bilal Abdullah, an emergency-room physician, into the security bollards at the entrance of Glasgow International Airport. Traveling at 30 miles per hour, the Jeep detonated on impact. The security barriers prevented the vehicle's penetration into the interior of the airport, and Ahmed was killed in the attack. Abdullah was later found guilty of conspiracy to commit murder and received a prison sentence of 32 years.

Terrorists who do not attract attention to themselves are the bigger concern. The 9/11 hijackers raised suspicion by wanting to learn how to take off and pilot an aircraft but showing no interest in learning how to land. But these were subtle clues that ultimately did not change the outcome. More openly demonstrative behaviors may suggest less formalized training, and perhaps a looser affiliation: jihad by inspiration rather than conscription. This is consistent with an Al Qaeda reinventing itself, often below the intelligence and investigative radar, as its strategic influence and recruitment efforts quietly intensify.

The new breed of Islamic jihadist will likely possess profile characteristics that make it more difficult to identify their affiliations and intent, observe their behaviors, and monitor them on an ongoing basis. They will be young, but they will also be on track to establish themselves in careers. They will be upwardly mobile, many of them, and work in the professions. The use of computers, computer tablets, smartphones, and social media will be second nature to them. Given that terrorists operate in secretive, almost anonymous cellular structures, communication over the Internet is important. The ability to organize using the Internet and tools of social media is important. In a word, the new terrorists will be cyber-enabled, and they will blend into the fabric of any country they live in, as well as their workplace. They will therefore become the ultimate insider threat.

 ## A CALL HEARD VAGUELY

Throughout the course of the Internet age, the nation has failed to predict the extent of the cyber threat, its association with the physical terrorist threat and the overwhelming, massive vulnerability of the Internet, an integration of technologies that were developed purposely not to have any security. Hackers weren't always taken seriously by industry. The 1983 movie *War Games* was the story of a student hacker who accidentally broke into a military computer system. But that was Hollywood. Although a few early hackers gained notoriety, most were perceived as somewhere between a benign nuisance and a criminal. A few actually thought about a cataclysmic event such as an electronic Pearl Harbor. They were not necessarily ignored, but it is fair to say that they were marginalized.

A few books sounded the warning of a terrorist threat and an attack on U.S. critical infrastructure. One of those books was *Black Ice: The Invisible Threat of Cyber-Terrorism*, by Dan Verton and published in 2003. As has been said, to everything there is a season. That was not the season. The attacks of 9/11 clearly showed critical infrastructure vulnerability, particularly in communications technology. Afterward, companies began to look more carefully at disaster recovery and business continuity planning. Still, it wasn't time. Now is the time, after so many trade secrets have been stolen, so many personal records compromised. But is it too late? And what is the real threat?

Much is being said and written about the concept of a lone wolf. It's interesting. In nature, a wolf kills when it is hungry or is threatened. Terrorists are not entirely lone wolves. Terrorists are indoctrinated; they are inspired. They may not receive from *Inspire* or directly from Al Qaeda a complete bomb-making kit. But is there a difference between inspiring someone to kill someone else and in handing them the tools necessary to make the kill? The answer is that in a court of law there may be a difference. In the court of public opinion the answer may be divided. To those who lost a friend or loved one, to those who experienced the physical and mental anguish of the Boston Marathon bombing and its aftermath, the subtlety is irrelevant.

Terrorist action, while extreme and loathsome, even barbaric, is typically well planned. It is an integrated plan backed by lethal impact and painstaking strategic consideration. While whether the Boston bombing was directly or indirectly connected to *Inspire* is an important consideration in many ways, it is the impact of the action, in the eye of the terrorist, that matters. The Tsarnaev brothers, and whoever else may have been engaged in their strike against the peaceful gathering of athletes and supporters on April 15, 2013, launched an attack that was heard around the world. *Inspire* may or may not have been the hands-on creator and promoter of it, but it will no doubt be the beneficiary of it.

Maybe an attack against the power grid or other target will not be made by Islamic fundamentalists, Al Qaeda finding such disruption disadvantageous. Maybe it will be a rogue government, such as Iran or North Korea, maybe Syria and its Syrian Electronic Army. It is well known that Iran has been digitally attacking banks, certainly targets of critical infrastructure. From the point of defense, it doesn't really matter whether the attack comes at the hands of the terrorist or the rogue nation-state or its military. Therefore the justification for investing in a strong cyber defense is that the threat is real, even profound. It should also be noted that critical infrastructure, given its broad definition, is almost certainly on the cyber target list.

In October 2009, the Department of Homeland Security opened the National Cybersecurity and Communications Integration Center. This 24-hour watch and warning center serves as the nation's principal hub for organizing cyber response efforts and maintaining the national cyber and communications common operational picture. DHS also works with the private sector, other government agencies, and the international community to mitigate risks by leveraging the tools, tradecraft, and techniques malicious actors use and converting them into actionable information for all 18 critical infrastructure sectors to use against cyber threats.

At the front lines vital partnerships have been forged with antivirus companies to take proactive measures to stop possible threats from reaching public- and private-sector partners by developing and sharing standardized threat indication, prevention, mitigation, and response information products with its .gov partners and constituents. This was accomplished by the U.S. Computer Emergency Readiness Team (US-CERT). In 2011, US-CERT responded to more than 106,000 incident reports and released more than 5,000 actionable cyber security alerts and information products to public- and private-sector partners.

In 2011, the DHS Industrial Control Systems Computer Emergency Response Team (ICS-CERT) conducted 78 assessments of control system entities, which helps the business community to identify security gaps and prioritize mitigation measures. DHS also empowers owners and operators by providing a cyber self-evaluation tool, which was utilized by over 1,000 companies in 2011, as well as in-person and online training sessions.

"The aggregation of large amounts of data that can potentially be accessed under one attack could cause both security liabilities and privacy liabilities for hundreds of insured policyholders simultaneously,"[4] says John B. Graham, a security and privacy subject matter expert at Zurich North America. "This same scenario could also mean direct harm to insured companies by causing interruptions to their operations, which could diminish their flow of income. For example, many insureds could end up using the same industry-leading cloud provider to store and manage the sensitive data of their customers. If that provider suffered a significant breach, are there adequate safeguards in place to prevent a large-scale impact to many insureds at the same time?" he wonders.

"Similarly, large-scale attacks against any of the 16 critical infrastructure sectors that can affect multiple insureds at once could cause interruptions to their operations," says Graham. "Can there really be a digital Pearl Harbor? Many experts don't think that's possible. If it's not feasible today, could it be feasible in two years or five years?"

A cyber by attack by terrorists is not always easily identifiable. Cyber attack is pretty much a continuous experience, and the identity of the attacker isn't always obvious. The constant probe attacks, in the form of cyber probes against critical infrastructure, could come from cyber criminals, nation-states intent on stealing information, or from hostile military forces. Such attacks may come from independent, unaffiliated hacker groups. Unless an attack originates with a known cyber terrorist group, or unless a terrorist group takes credit for an attack, reliable identification is complex and not always possible.

 ## ATTACK UPON ATTACK, NO PEACE IN SIGHT

In part the issue is the sheer number of cyber attacks taking place at any given time. These attacks are against critical infrastructure, government offices, and private-sector companies outside the defense contractor network and critical infrastructure.

According to Nextgov (www.nextgov.com), the United Kingdom receives 120,000 attacks daily. The state of Utah sustains about 20 million attack attempts a day, up from 1 million a day several years ago. But no one really knows how many are directly attributable to cyber terrorist attacks. Then again, all could be considered terrorist attacks.

One thing is certain: The current state of preparedness against a dizzying array of critical infrastructure targets is not what it needs to be. That is not only disappointing, it is dangerous.

In many ways, it seems astounding how fast technology has evolved and how fully it has been embraced, for purposes good and bad. We have figured out to make most any activity subject to some type of Internet application. Yet the ability to secure that activity has fallen far short of where it needs to be. Undeniably, more security exists today than two decades ago, when Mr. Schwartau addressed Congress. But that's not the point. A number of security and privacy regulations have been introduced into the marketplace. More standards and guidelines exist. But what has been lost is advantage. It doesn't matter that the United States was behind the development of the Internet. It doesn't matter that the many products and services associated with the Internet were created from U.S. capital and ingenuity. None of this matters. What does matter is the vulnerability of virtually every industry built upon an Internet-enabled foundation. That means that it is accessible by anyone with the will and the talent to break into it. That's the bad news. The worse news is that the number of those with the will and the skills to break into it is growing exponentially.

 NOTES

1. Presidential Policy Directive 21, February 12, 2013, www.whitehouse.gov/the-press-office/2013/02/12/presidential-policy-directive-critical-infrastructure-security-and-resil.
2. InfoWarCon Conference, Brussels, Belgium, January 1996.
3. MacDonnell Ulsch, *Threat! Managing Risk in a Hostile World* (Altamonte Springs, FL: Institute of Internal Auditors Research Foundation, 2008).
4. Author conversation with John Graham, Zurich North America, November 2013.

PART II

Corporate Vulnerabilities in the Digital Society

Prepare to Defend Yourself and Your Brand

CHAPTER FOUR

What Is the True Cost of a Cyber Attack?

Cyber attacks have become common occurrences. The companies in our study experienced 343 successful attacks per week and 1.4 successful attacks per company per week. We found that the average annualized cost of cyber crime for 234 organizations in our study is $7.2 million per year, with a range of $375,387 to $58 million. This represents an increase in cost of 30 percent from the consolidated global results of last year's cyber cost study.

—*Dr. Larry Ponemon of the Ponemon Institute*

ERE'S A frightening thought. It's an observation, actually, one from the U.S. Office of the National Counterintelligence Executive. The U.S. workforce will experience a cultural shift that places greater value on access to information and less emphasis on privacy and data protection. At the same time, deepening globalization of economic activities will make national boundaries less of a deterrent to economic espionage than ever. The office further observes that political or social activists may use the tools of economic espionage against U.S. companies, agencies, or other entities, with disgruntled insiders leaking information about corporate trade secrets or critical U.S. technology to "hacktivist" groups like WikiLeaks.

It is an observation that's hard to argue with.

There is greater access to data, that's for sure. Not only is there more data today than ever before, but companies are keeping more of it (Big Data) and there are more places where data resides: more mobile devices, web sites, social media forums, and so on. And more people work remotely, from home, from hotels, even while on vacation. More people, using more data, on more devices, in more places, more of the time—and more people trying to steal the information. This is happening now, and the trend will continue. The scenario is decidedly not encouraging. Surely the convergence of these trends is going to result in greater breach-related costs. And there's an additional reason, too. Enhancing information security as part of an overall operational risk management isn't where it needs to be. This is unfortunate, but it's true.

All of this adds up to more data breaches, and that means more companies and governments spending more budget either on preventing or reducing breach impact, or paying the price after a breach occurs. It is usually the latter. While it is almost always less costly to prevent an information breach, organizations have not proven to be effective defenders of information integrity.

Try to avoid a data breach! That's the best advice. Preventing such a loss of information and brand integrity is always preferable, on many levels, to being the victim of a breach. It's also a lot less costly to prevent a breach. Sadly, it seems that some breaches are not preventable. This may sound fatalistic, but it's true. How could it be otherwise? Breaking and entering is not preventable. Homicide and other violent crimes are not preventable. It is possible to reduce these crimes, but crime cannot be eliminated. Crimes associated with cyber attacks are no different. It is critical to prepare for a breach, and how to respond to one, before it hits. Because when it hits, the meter starts running, and sometimes it doesn't stop for a long time.

Cyber attack frequency is rising, and they're increasingly effective (that is, damaging and costly). Examining the trends contributing to the frequency and effectiveness of the attacks, we see a "similarity between the tools, tactics, and techniques used by various actors, which reduces the reliability of using these factors to identify those responsible for computer network intrusions," according to the U.S. Office of the National Counterintelligence Executive. "Hacker websites are prevalent across the Internet, and tool sharing is common, causing intrusions by unrelated actors to exhibit similar technical characteristics."[1] This is a major contributor to the increase in costs globally. It is harder to differentiate, detect, and identify specific attackers because of these blending attacker signatures.

Another contributing factor in accurate detection is that many hackers route operations through computers in third countries or physically operate from third countries to obscure the origin of their activity. This process of redirecting attacks through third countries adds a veil of obfuscation in identifying the hackers' origin. Additional time is required to make the identification, and at additional cost in terms of identification, remediation, and recovery. It may also give the hackers more time to steal additional information, which can result in greater costs, financial and otherwise. To further complicate identification of the attackers, the foreign intelligence services of other countries may also be integrated into the attack scenario. Such attacks, which happen swiftly and are subject to rapid change, make it even harder to identify the attacker. At a macro level, it also complicates law enforcement investigation and delays action against the attacker. Again, there is a cost associated with this, and taxpayers foot the bill.

There's no sense in playing games. A cyber breach is going to be costly—in a lot of ways. There's the actual cost of the attack, which may involve the theft of money, extortion, and so on. And then there is the long chain of associated costs that are the unavoidable consequence of such an event. Consider the cyber attacks against companies like Target at the end of 2013. As with many similar breaches, the effects of these attacks are often not readily apparent, and the damage does not end immediately. Sometimes the attacks persist. But the aftermath of these attacks often has a long tail. The impact can be substantial and enduring. Some observers believe that the Target breach will ultimately bear a price tag of $1 billion, perhaps more. This isn't an unreasonable prediction. Take the TJX data breach. It happened in 2007 and is still talked about. Not only does the talk about data breaches linger, but the costs can continue to add up. Many of the data breaches seen in the pages of the media today will suffer long lives and involve a lot of costs.

Cost can be measured in many ways. There's the actual loss associated with a breach: money stolen, for example. There's the cost of managing and remediating the breach and its aftermath. Then consider the cost of lost revenue associated with customer drift. There's the loss of value of the company stock, the loss or hesitancy of business alliance partners and distribution partners. All of these losses and costs add up to loss and uncertainty about the future. Often it is difficult to calculate the cost in the short term because the impact of a cyber breach can be lingering, often for years.

What does it really cost when a company sustains a cyber attack? A lot of statistics have been published about the cost of cyber attacks. But there are many ways to answer the question. As is so often the case, what sounds like a straightforward question should have a straightforward answer. Unfortunately, that is not the case. Rational metrics exist for trying to better understand the costs of an attack, but these are only guidelines. In reality, the answer can be complicated, with many elements pertinent to the calculus absent during the analysis.

One thing, though, is clear. As the Ponemon study noted, cyber crime is growing—and it is costly. Ponemon found that U.S. companies are much more likely to experience the most expensive types of cyber attacks: malicious code, denial of service, and Web-based incidents. Similarly, Australia is most likely to experience denial-of-service attacks. In contrast, German companies are least likely to experience malicious code and botnets, according to Ponemon. Japanese companies are least likely to experience stolen devices and malicious code attacks.

Both short-term and long-term considerations have to be included in the assessment of cost. Sometimes it takes years to calculate the cost of a breach. Why? Because cyber attacks, like many other crimes, occur episodically, and over extended periods. Discovery timeframes vary. Some attacks are hit-and-run attacks: The damage occurs, it is immediately identified, and the incident investigation begins immediately.

It is never a good idea to wait for the middle of a breach to formulate an incident response plan. But this does happen, and often. It almost always costs more. Planning for a breach is prudent not only in order to defend a company's reputation and its obligations to its customer base, but from a cost perspective as well. Every stage of response has a cost associated with it, and planning each phase of the response results in a judicious and fiscally responsible risk management approach. Detection, investigation, incident response, containment, recovery, and other postbreach issues can be expensive.

 ## CYBER ATTACK DETECTION SOMETIMES TAKES YEARS

Denial-of-service attacks are often protracted and may occur at various times, often to create the greatest level of disruption and inconvenience.

Other, more covert, attacks take place over years: The victim fails to realize that attacks are occurring. These cyber attacks can be subtle, hard to detect, based upon the ability of the attacked company to detect them. Some well-defended organizations can recognize attack signals early on. Others don't have a clue, often for very long periods, even years. This highlights the importance of creating and managing an environment that is technically sophisticated and current. Companies with antiquated information technology systems and those that fail to adequately monitor for attack signals are the most vulnerable. Make no mistake about it, the longer it takes to detect the breach, the greater the potential for damage, and the greater the potential for damage, the greater the cost, on many fronts.

Also, some companies may monitor extensively, but then fail to analyze and correlate data that would indicate that the company is under attack, either from inside the organization or from the outside. This can be an inflammatory situation. Technology was used to capture the data but no one really looked at it carefully. Depending on the specific predicament, this can be a violation of various regulations, especially for regulated markets such as health care and financial services.

There are companies that have been successfully penetrated because the enterprise operating system was aged, no longer supported optimally by the developer. It no longer receives the appropriate software patches and upgrades. Sometimes this vulnerability arises due to lack of awareness and understanding by the board of directors and even by executive management. Management and the directors often have a faulty view of technology. Their perspectives have a long history. Since the dawn of the information technology age, information technology has best been interpreted as the use of tools to increase productivity. That's why there's an information technology industry. However, things have gotten more complicated. Information technology is also a vulnerability, which makes it a risk. It seems like a simple thing to comprehend, yet many do not.

But think about it this way: If a management team or board envisions information technology exclusively as a tool of productivity, and employees are adequately productive, it may be interpreted that there is no need to upgrade the information technology system. That translates into a condition of inadequate defensive protections based on the fact that the older technology is no longer supported. That older technology may be perfectly adequate for the employees to do the more visible part of their jobs, but it may be grossly inadequate from an information integrity and defense perspective. This was a board of directors' decision. They felt it unnecessary to invest in an enterprise-wide upgrade. The company was breached over a period of years and no one knew it, until it was too late, the damage done. The cost of the breach, as measured over the breach investigation period, was considerable. But the actual long-term cost is harder to assess. Here's why, and this is a common condition. Such conditions have contributed to serious breaches. First, the cyber attacks were not identifiable. Second, the malicious software was not prevented from extracting restricted information from the company.

Often, from the board's postbreach view, there's the recognition that the money should have been invested.

ONE OF THE FIRST QUESTIONS: "HOW MUCH WILL THIS COST?"

The history of breach investigations is rich with a lot of questions—and fewer answers—about the true cost impact of the event. When a breach is discovered, often the first words out of the mouth of the executive charged with the responsibility of managing the breach are, "How much is this going to cost?" Most often, the answer is this: "That's a good question. There's a great deal of uncertainly. The facts are unknown. We'll know more soon, but we may not know the full extent of the damage for some time, and maybe a very long time." The attacked then asks, "Can you define 'some time'?" To which the answer can be, "It may be weeks, it may be years, before we know the whole story. Or some answers may be unobtainable."

The short answer is this: it's hard to say, and it depends on when you stop counting, because some breaches have a long tail.

Many variables exist that can influence what is known, when it is known, whether that factor will influence the cost, and when that cost will be incurred. The victim's response is understandable. Regardless of the crisis at hand, most anyone wants to know what is happening, how it happened, and whether it is still happening. Sometimes it isn't easy to determine if an attack is still under way. In other cases, especially if a company is being targeted in an ongoing cyber attack, such as a denial-of-service attack, the costs continue to mount.

That's one thing about the different types of cyber attacks. Some attacks occur once, some periodically, other continuously. Many breaches are comprised of multiple phases, each with a cost impact. The commonality that companies experience in these attacks is the unknown. No one likes it, everyone experiences it. Unknowns also interject questions about cost.

Then there is usually another question that follows, frequently in the first minutes or hours of the case: "Are we going to have report this?" The answer is typically something like this: "More than likely, you will have to report it to somebody at some time. It may be your corporate customer, the state, federal, and even foreign regulators, but, yes, you will have to report this to someone." The answer, of course, is in the requirements of the statutes and regulations, as well as the contract language between the parties. In the case of a breach of unregulated data, there is still most likely the obligation to report the event to others with a vested interest: business partners, investors, bankers, shareholders, and others. Of course, all of this takes time and adds substantially to the cost of the breach.

A FEW COMMON COST FACTORS

Even for companies that are insured against the loss of information integrity, the cost can be considerable. One of the variables is how much insurance is carried and what exactly the policies cover. Then there are companies that have insurance but choose not to file a claim. Why? Because of concern over an increase in insurance rates.

Here are some common factors regarding cyber attack cost business impact:

- The attack isn't recognized in a timely manner, which often occurs. There is a great deal of variance in detection timelines. Inadequate detection technology is an issue, but so is the type of attack. An attack intended to shut down a web site will be noticed more quickly than a surreptitious attack designed to quietly steal valuable information.
- Attack indicators are not properly interpreted as a cyber attack and there's no sense of urgency or immediacy, leading to the loss of precious time.
- The first inclination may be to manage the attack internally, using only internal resources, which is often an inadequate approach, leading to the loss of precious investigative time and adding cost.

- Law enforcement may or may not become actively engaged. Law enforcement engagement can be a cost consideration, because an investigation paid for by law enforcement does not have a direct negative financial impact on the company. However, the principal purpose of a law enforcement investigation is to develop a case for prosecution, not to act as an advocate for the breached company. Law enforcement determines the extent and immediacy of its involvement based on several factors, among them the threat to national security, a direct financial loss exceeding a threshold amount, and other factors such as the involvement of transnational organized crime and human or sexual trafficking.

- There is a lack of awareness of the probability of attack. Many boards still consider cyber attack as a "technology thing" or a "security thing." They don't consider it a "board thing." This contributes to an environmental apathy throughout the enterprise, one that may result in deficiencies in a variety of defenses that can quickly and accurately identify cyber attacks.

- Decision paralysis is another factor. Many breaches are never reported, either to regulators or customers or even business partners, for one reason or another. Sometimes it is difficult for executives to report breaches. It can lead to significant cost and loss of brand value and reputation, and breaches can end up bringing a company into protracted, costly litigation. Thus some executives will wait to disclose, or not disclose at all. In either scenario, the failure to act aggressively to stop the attack and at the same time begin remediating the damage and potential future damage can be damaging. In the failure to disclose to the appropriate parties a cyber attack and resulting data breach, executives sometimes are just hoping for the best.

- In the case of some external service providers, while they may report the breach to clients, they might not be fully cooperative with the clients beyond the basic minimum requirements of reporting consistent and in accordance with state and federal or even foreign-country regulations. This leads to substantial additional effort—and risk—on the part of the principal company. That translates into additional cost.

 WHAT ABOUT UNREPORTED BREACHES?

Who wants to do business with a company that is constantly breached by hackers? Doing so could increase the risk to a customer, personal or corporate. But then how does anyone know if there's been a breach if it isn't reported? Many breaches are never reported. Some of those incidents should be reported because they are required to be under law. Still, many are not. Actual levels of compliance are believed by many regulators to be quite low. And what about the cyber attacks that result in the theft of intellectual property and trade secrets? Such attacks are not usually reported to regulators. So ascertaining reputation cost is very difficult under the best of circumstances.

The Office of the National Counterintelligence Executive states that:

- Many victims of economic espionage are unaware of the crime until years after loss of the information.
- Even when a company knows its sensitive information has been stolen by an insider or that its computer networks have been penetrated, it may choose not to report the event to the FBI or other law enforcement agencies. No legal requirement to report a loss of sensitive information or a remote computer intrusion exists, and announcing a security breach of this kind could tarnish a company's reputation and endanger its relationships with investors, bankers, suppliers, customers, and other stakeholders.
- A company also may not want to publicly accuse a corporate rival or foreign government of stealing its secrets from fear of offending potential customers or business partners.
- Finally, it is inherently difficult to assign an economic value to some types of information that are subject to theft. It would, for example, be nearly impossible to estimate the monetary value of talking points for a meeting between officials from a U.S. company and foreign counterparts.[2]

While companies may be required to report a breach of regulated data, such as health care information or other personal or financial data, very few companies actually track the fully dimensioned cost of a cyber attack over the long term. While the cyber theft of personal and health information captures the headlines, the theft of intellectual property and trade secrets can have severe long-term consequences, including reputation risk and cost. Under most circumstances, there is no obligation to report the loss of business information to law enforcement or other government agencies.

Economic espionage is growing and has a substantial cost impact on companies in the United States and elsewhere. Many companies don't discover these thefts until months or even years later.

Here's a rational scenario: Say a company pins its financial hopes and future on a critical technology. That specific technology will be the foundation for growth, revenue, profits, and the capability to perhaps acquire competitors, compete more effectively in the market, be able to afford more aggressive marketing and sales efforts, and build and sustain a market presence and even market dominance.

Let's say that the company has a partner in the development of that technology. Maybe that partner is a venture capital firm, a bank, or another company or companies committing resources to the successful completion and deployment of that technology. For argument's sake, say the total investment is $100 million. Assume that the $100 million investment is intended to generate, over 10 years, $1 billion. But the technology is compromised, stolen by a nation-state competitor, who is able to use the technology to leapfrog over the rest of the competitors, including the developers of the technology. What might be the consequence?

For one, there is the loss of projected revenue and market position, and everything that comes with being in the position of market dominance. A loss of market value could occur, based on market confidence, with devalued stock performance. If any of the technology loss was covered by insurance, insurance premiums would no doubt increase. The partners engaged in the development of the technology could sever relations with the company or, worse, sever and sue for the losses. It may prove difficult to repay any bank loans, just as it may prove difficult to find technology, financial, and market partners in the future. Then consider that the company's information systems were compromised and must be repaired and then be better protected in the future.

Will the board blame the chief executive officer? That has happened before, and it will happen again. After all, someone is going to have to take the blame. Senior executives and boards of directors are becoming savvy enough about cyber attacks to know that these attacks don't just happen, that there is usually someone to blame. The blame has historically been placed on the senior security officer, sometimes the chief information officer. But as executives and board members learn more about cyber attacks, they are coming to grips with the basic fact that successful cyber attacks usually happen because of lack of awareness by employees of the threat of risky behaviors, antiquated technology, ineffective information management policies and procedures that need to be revisited, and the failure to comply with even the basic mandatory minimums associated with regulations intended to reduce the risk of compromise of personal information. Applying even these basics to the protection of intellectual property and trade secrets is better than not protecting that information. But not all executives and all companies are coming up to speed quickly enough. And all the while, cyber attack sophistication is rising.

 ## CYBER ATTACKS RESULT IN A WIDER IMPACT: THE COMMUNITY

The cost of cyber attacks can also be measured in terms of loss to the community. While most unfortunate, severe breaches, ones that result in the full impact of regulatory, legal, financial, and reputation risk, have formidable consequences. Employees lose jobs. The breached company pays less in taxes because it may be generating less revenue. Those jettisoned employees are paying less income tax because they are making less, and they may also be also drawing unemployment insurance and perhaps additional government entitlements such as subsidized health care. Municipalities are impacted because it becomes more difficult for homeowners to pay real estate taxes. The felt impact chain seems relentless and unending, yet these concerns are seldom part of the cyber breach impact discussion.

Even without a cyber breach to blame, the United States felt this kind of impact in the financial crash of 2007–2008. Most cyber attacks may not have this kind of highly consequential result. But on a smaller scale, it is worth considering the holistic impact that these types of breaches may have on the people who work for the breached companies.

Putting this in perspective, consider that stolen intellectual property and trade secrets bring a great deal of complexity to the question of determining the cost of a breach. Though it is difficult to place an absolute financial loss on breached intellectual property and trade secrets, consider that the total value of compromised secrets is possibly $1 trillion a year. The U.S. government estimates that approximately $250 billion to $300 billion a year is lost by U.S. companies through economic espionage.

Germany's Federal Office for the Protection of the Constitution (BfV) estimates that German companies lose $28–$71 billion and 30,000–70,000 jobs per year from foreign economic espionage. Approximately 70 percent of cases involve insiders.

South Korea says that the costs from foreign economic espionage in 2008 were $82 billion, up from $26 billion in 2004. The South Koreans report that 60 percent of victims are small and medium-size businesses and that half of all economic espionage comes from China.

Japan's Ministry of Economy, Trade, and Industry conducted a survey of 625 manufacturing firms in late 2007 and found that more than 35 percent of those responding reported some form of technology loss. More than 60 percent of those leaks involved China.

The important consideration is to recognize that cyber attacks have consequences, and those consequences can be measured in financial and other terms. It is not often the case that cyber breaches stimulate this track of thought, maybe because there is no one type of cyber attack. There is no one-size-fits-all cyber attack model. Every breach is different. Each company, based on its level of preparedness and defenses, is impacted to a greater or lesser degree. It matters what is being protected: regulated personal information or business secrets. It also matters, from a cost perspective, how long it takes before the breach is discovered. Some are identified rather swiftly, while others are discovered months or years later. The ability to identify cyber attackers sooner rather than later is based on several criteria: the technology in place to detect attacks, which is a direct reflection of the commitment and investment in that capability, and the level of sophistication of those attempting to penetrate the implemented defense.

The best advice is to try and prevent breaches by investing appropriately in the operational risk management processes and practices that will reduce the likelihood of a breach or the impact of one. Some organizations assume that breaches won't hit them. Maybe a few of them will be proven right. But most will be proven wrong.

Some have asked, "Well, what companies have gone out of business because of a breach?" Or they will ask, "What company stock has suffered because of a breach?" These are reasonable questions. The first answer is this: Don't let the past be a guide. We live in a rapidly changing environment. Just because it didn't happen in the past doesn't mean that it won't happen in the future. But there's another part of the answer. Since many breaches are never reported, their impacts do not become public. This is the shark fin perception. Reported breaches are like shark fins. Visual conformation of a shark fin gives rise to caution. Reported breaches are the visible representations of what we perceive about the threat and its result. But it's the body of the shark, beneath the surface, that is the real threat, and that is what we don't see until it is too late. This is like the unreported breach. We don't really know what it looks like, who did it, why it was done, or what the impact will be. We don't know because there is no visual representation of it. It may as well be invisible. Basing our perceptions about hacking on what is available in the press is misleading and even dangerous. Most breaches are simply never reported, so the visible truth is not consistent with the factual truth. And that's the factual truth.

 NOTES

1. Office of the National Counterintelligence Executive, "Foreign Spies Stealing US Economic Secrets in Cyberspace: Report to Congress on Foreign Economic Collection and Industrial Espionage, 2009–2011," October 2011, www.ncix .gov/publications/reports/fecie_all/Foreign_Economic_Collection_2011.pdf.
2. Ibid.

CHAPTER FIVE

U.S. Cyber Public Policy

Don't Rely on It to Protect the Brand

We the People of the United States, in Order to form a more perfect Union, establish Justice, insure domestic Tranquility, provide for the common defence, promote the general Welfare, and secure the Blessings of Liberty to ourselves and our Posterity, do ordain and establish this Constitution for the United States of America.

—*The U.S. Constitution*

I N A world compromised by the certainty and intensity of the current cyber threat, it is reasonable to require the government to provide for the common cyber defense. Little did the founding fathers conceive of a society and an economy driven not by agriculture and local trade but by invisible electrons traversing the planet and carrying a diverse array of information that fuels the engines of international commerce. How could they have known that enemies of the people and of the state could somehow in the years ahead easily, equally invisibly, and more quickly than the blink of an eye snatch that valuable information out of thin air and turn it to their advantage as if they were the alchemists of some future era?

In fighting against the cyber threat, whether in the form of terrorism, crime, economic espionage, or another scenario, the government of the United States and other governments around the world have an obligation to protect and defend. But that is a complicated mission. No one country is going to defeat the cyber threat. Public policy, though, demands that the United States drive a stake in the heart of cyber defense. The common cyber defense is distributed across various organizations throughout the government. The Federal Bureau of Investigation, Central Intelligence Agency, National Security Agency, Drug Enforcement Administration, Department of the Treasury, Department of Homeland Security, Department of Justice, and Department of Defense as well as each of the military branches play roles in combating the cyber threat. And there are other agencies in the fight. Health and Human Services regulates the protection of health care, and various other regulators are engaged in consumer financial protection, including the Federal Trade Commission. The Internet Crime Complaint Center, or IC3, is an import element of cyber defense, a partnership between the FBI and the National White Collar Crime Center (NW3C).

The federal government has a substantial investment in defending against the cyber threat. However, that threat is extremely diversified. The threat is not flagged—it is not a nation or even some specified natural geographic territory. The cyber threat is intriguing. In some ways, it is like a firearm with a military application: It can be used as a weapon of offense or defense. It can be used to rob banks, or to steal health care records. The Internet can be used to steal information of any kind. It can also be the tip of the spear in an attack on vital infrastructure, from electric utilities to the transfer of money to the distribution of food and supplies of all kinds— a digital force multiplier. Clearly, providing for the common cyber defense is mandatory. The military and the intelligence community use the Internet as a tool of offense and defense. The government has a role in the cyber defense.

But what role? The evidence suggests that the approach to combating the cyber threat is not working.

Executive Order 13636, Improving Critical Infrastructure Cybersecurity, appeared in the media a lot in 2013. The executive order acknowledges that "the cyber threat to critical infrastructure continues to grow and represents one of the most serious national security challenges we must confront."

Critical infrastructure is comprised of a number of sectors necessary for the country to operate under reasonably normal conditions. Here's the fundamental issue: Most critical infrastructure operations are connected to the Internet. They are therefore vulnerable. One of the problems with the executive order is that it is an executive order. On the other hand, does the nation really want more laws that mandate how things will be secured?

Not having suffered a massive power outage that spans the nation slows any appreciation for an equally massive undertaking to prevent a digital attack of this magnitude. Not having felt the sting of money ceasing to transit through the wires, or of food not being distributed as it has been, uninterrupted, for decades, any sense of urgency falters. While most experts agree that extreme vulnerabilities exist and are likely to result in disruption or inconvenience on a potentially large scale, the appetite to aggressively pursue the matter is not there. This is not a grassroots issue that translates easily into the everyday life of America or any other country. Perhaps it should be, but the Internet isn't warm and fuzzy, and although many use it, they don't understand its connectivity to daily lives beyond not getting texts, e-mail, surfing, and social media pursuits. Issues larger and more immediate gain greater attention. Yes, there are news reports about credit card data theft, an inconvenience for sure, but few consumers are left out in the cold. A bank is hit by cyber criminals? Again, no bank customers were shot in the holdup.

There are 12 sections in the executive order. In Section 7, Baseline Framework to Reduce Cyber Risk to Critical Infrastructure, the order requires that "the Secretary of Commerce shall direct the Director of the National Institute of Standards and Technology (the 'Director') to lead the development of a framework to reduce cyber risks to critical infrastructure (the 'Cybersecurity Framework'). The Cybersecurity Framework shall include a set of standards, methodologies, procedures, and processes that align policy, business, and technological approaches to address cyber risks."

That's a tall order, executive or not. It's also a necessary order. But converting a large program such as this into a working solution to the problem is difficult at best. Translation: It is unlikely to happen. As the framework states, "The Cybersecurity Framework shall incorporate voluntary consensus standards and industry best practices to the fullest extent possible. The Cybersecurity Framework shall be consistent with voluntary international standards when such international standards will advance the objectives of this order, and shall meet the requirements of the National Institute of Standards and Technology Act." The key word defining the initiative is "voluntary."

NO GUARANTEES WITH THIS EXECUTIVE ORDER

Interestingly, there are no guarantees for the continued development of the program, or so it seems. Section 12, General Provisions, states that the program is to be implemented "subject to the availability of appropriations."

The president "directed NIST to work with stakeholders to develop a voluntary framework for reducing cyber risks to critical infrastructure," according to the National Institute of Standards and Technology. "The Framework will consist of standards, guidelines, and best practices to promote the protection of critical infrastructure. The prioritized, flexible, repeatable, and cost-effective approach of the framework will help owners and operators of critical infrastructure to manage cybersecurity-related risk while protecting business confidentiality, individual privacy and civil liberties."

President Obama remarked on February 12, 2013, in a speech from the White House, that "we can achieve these goals through a partnership with the owners and operators of critical infrastructure to improve cyber security information sharing and collaboratively develop and implement risk-based standards."

If there is to be an answer to the question of how cyber attacks must be met, then surely that answer is this: Government and the private corporate sector must work together, nations must work cooperatively, and every user of the Internet must take personal responsibility. And if there is a myth that abounds, it is that public policy and legislation that results in regulation will solve this complicated issue.

Is it necessary to pass laws and create regulations to implement those laws with respect to protecting personal information? It does seem that way. Is there value in the government working with the private sector in order to better protect a wide range of information, from personal information to trade secrets to the national defense? The answer is yes, but cooperation is no silver bullet. There is no silver bullet. Nevertheless, cooperation between governments and the private sector is essential. It's just that expectation levels need to be established regarding the result of such cooperation, because to date the issues remain clouded, the level of true cooperation less than compelling.

It's time for truth telling. The government needs to hear it, and so does the private sector. The track record of information protection has not been one to brag about. Media headlines every day illustrate the level of compromise. Fifty million credit cards breached here, 100 million breached there. Nation-states stealing technology over the Internet and through foreign nationals based in the United States. From most any perspective, the magnitude of information loss and theft has been frightful, whether we are talking about the U.S. federal government or about industry. Few industries have escaped the swift cyber sword—banks, investment firms, pharmaceutical companies, manufacturers, product development companies, utilities, defense contractors, and other interests.

Working cooperatively requires trust, or at least a high degree of it. To date, there's reason to doubt. No one seems immune. It is no one person's fault, no one agency or one company.

The breach of classified data by Edward Snowden, the NSA contractor employed by a private firm, has brought the issue of information protection and third-party vendors to a new high point, which is actually a low point in terms of information integrity. In this case there was someone with privileged access, who was subjected to a reportedly deficient background investigation, who was able to violate most every basic security tenet and then fled the country. A hearing on Capitol Hill in June 2013 brought the issue into sharp, bitter, and even disturbing focus. That hard focus was delivered by perhaps an unlikely messenger, Senator Jon Tester, a third-generation Montana farmer with a degree in music, who butchers his own meat and carries it with him in carry-on luggage to Washington, D.C. He also serves on the Homeland Security Committee. The subject of the Senate hearing was "Safeguarding Our Nation's Secrets."[1]

The senator from Montana said, "Recent events have forced us all to take a close look at the programs carried out by this government in the name of national security." He was referring, of course, to the Snowden affair. He stated that it was necessary "to raise critical questions about how our government is vetting the individuals, whether they are Federal employees or contractors, who have access to our Nation's most sensitive data." The same may be said of corporate executives and members of the board of directors. How are these company titans making sure that their organizations don't hire someone who will disclose critical secrets?

Some will argue that such vetting is the responsibility of human resources, or security, maybe risk management, but certainly not the board of directors. Yet look at the impact the Snowden affair has had. The government made a huge error. Companies make these errors, too. The goal is to protect the brand, not to delegate what some executives may think is not worthy of their consideration. That's a bad call.

Senator Tester raised an issue that should be addressed by any executive with fiduciary responsibility, every executive whose decisions contribute to or detract from corporate value and the defense of the brand. The issue is results and accountability. Too often these issues are sidelined.

A week before the hearing, Senator Tester asked General Keith Alexander, the director of the NSA, whose operation had been compromised by Snowden, "a straightforward question. After the outcry of WikiLeaks, after the presidential executive order calling for improved classified network security, and after spending tens if not hundreds of billions of taxpayer dollars to keep outsiders from accessing our nation's secrets, how in the world does a contractor, who had been on the job for less than three months, get his hands on information detailing a highly classified government program that he subsequently shared with foreign media outlets?"

That's a fair question. How many executives are asking this kind of question as they consider the defense of their brand? The follow-up question is, How many are asking that question before a breach occurs, rather than after the damage has been done? The answer is that far too few executives are asking this question before the breach.

If the actions of Snowden had taken place in a publicly traded company, the outcry would have been palpable. Heads would have rolled. But the damage would have been done, and a significant element of that damage would be the reputation of the organization—the brand.

"The long answer is one that we will ultimately require a great deal of soul searching by the folks in this room and throughout the government," said Senator Tester. "But the short answer is that, in terms of securing classified information, we just do not have an external problem; we have an internal one." He's right. The problem is not just in the government. The insider threat from employees and third-party contractors is huge. The reason is that, at least in part, the insider is just that: an insider. They are the beneficiaries of a certain level of trust. They are colleagues. Most workers do not think that colleagues are a threat. Colleagues are to be trusted.

Senator Tester went on to say that the government must "examine the efficiency and effectiveness of the security clearance process." It's unsettling that many in the private sector fail to adequately apply this same standard to managing the reputation of the brand. Understanding who is in a given environment is part of the process of knowing whom to trust and in managing brand reputation. But, again, this is a process often crafted at lower levels of the organization, even though failures in the process threaten the brand.

GOVERNMENT-INDUSTRY COOPERATION: NO SILVER BULLET

The government has not yet identified the right process for better risk management, which is why, to at least some extent, cooperation between the public and private sectors, while potentially helpful, is not that silver bullet. Managing risk must be a collaborative process, as much as it must be an individual approach. Reliance upon regulation and government oversight is not the answer, yet it is perceived to be the answer by companies that make the potentially fatal assumption that complying with regulations makes them secure. While the aim of the government may be to protect and defend, the reality is often far different.

In that same hearing with Senator Tester, Senator Claire McCaskill of Missouri raised an interesting point. More than 90 percent of the background investigations done for government employees and contractors are conducted by the U.S. Office of Personnel Management, not third-party contractors. The government process, as are many in industry, is flawed, even seriously flawed.

Said Senator McCaskill, the committee's research "portrays a government agency where there is fraud, limited accountability, and no respect for taxpayer dollars. Conducting and managing background investigations costs the federal government over $1 billion per year." And what is the return on that investment? This is the question that executives and boards need to ask. The government has demonstrated that it has serious woes in managing information. But is industry doing any better? Not really. This is one area in which industry and government share much. It's just that the actions of government strike with an extremely wide swath and the impact can be felt by an entire nation.

Senator McCaskill was "shocked to learn" that the fund associated with the Office of Personnel Management used for conducting background investigations had never been audited. While the inspector general had attempted to conduct an audit, "The agency simply does not have or keep records that would allow him to do an audit." This raises the issue of whether companies are auditing third-party vendor firms conducting background investigations. In any case, it is clearly not a best practice.

Since 2007, 18 investigators have been convicted of falsifying investigations. "There are more than 40 other active and pending investigations into fabricated investigations, and it is possible that there are far more," the senator said. Such an admission certainly calls into question the efficacy of the program, as well as the legitimacy of it. How many employees at private companies conducting background investigations have been falsifying investigations? How many corporate clients of these background investigation firms have even asked the question?

Senator McCaskill remarked that these failures are "a reminder that background investigations have real consequences for our national security." And for the corporate brand.

In the same hearing, Senator Rob Portman of Ohio said, "The security clearance process, performed well, is critical because it ensures that our nation's most valuable information is protected while ensuring that we have the necessary personnel to conduct the duties that we need to have them out there doing to protect our country. Done poorly, it can be incredibly damaging. We run the risk of damaging leaks, hamstringing our agencies' abilities to fulfill their missions, as we have seen in cases over the last couple years, harming our allies and our ability to build alliances around the world." The same may also be said of any company's failure to ensure the integrity of the process.

Voluntary programs are often doomed to failure. Regulatory mandates help but are not generally successful, though regulations do establish a basic minimum requirement, which is better than nothing. Still, even mandated compliance levels are low, and even when compliance works, various regulations can seem contradictory and vary significantly from state to state and from one nation to the next. International cooperation is complicated. Obeying the rules internationally sounds great, but then reality interferes. Economic competition trumps strict adherence to the rules. Is it likely that China or other level-one economic competitors are going to stop using the Internet for domestic gain and international penetration of competitor sites? Visions of "one digital world" may sound appealing, but that is an unlikely scenario. It is not going to happen. Rooms full of diplomats pontificating about trade agreements and the economy and the state of relations are not going to result in the cessation of digital surveillance and information theft. Setting national goals, and then pursuing those goals as participants in the global economy, does not typically include detailed discussions of what is fair or just outside of domestic interests. This is neither criticism nor endorsement. It is simply reality.

 ## THE CHALLENGE OF DEFINING CYBER PUBLIC POLICY

Defining public policy within the context of the cyber threat is challenging. A lot of energy and money is being invested in devising a comprehensive solution, and a lot of intellectual cycles are being burned as the threat intensifies. The U.S. government is doing a lot of the right things in the cyber defense, but the problem is immensely complex. There's also the issue that government is not doing everything right either. Perhaps expectations of the government are too high. How much is enough? Borrowing from the comic strip character Pogo, it is fair to say that "we have met the enemy and he is us."

The Internet wars are pervasive and multidimensional and consist of many elements: offensive strikes against military targets, state-sponsored espionage, industrial espionage, transnational organized crime, money laundering, personal information theft, credit card theft, medical records theft. Rogue insiders compromise data and systems. Malicious intent and administrative errors seem to be the norm. The cyber threat affects everyone: individuals, families, cities, companies, organizations, governments; little remains untouched by its impact, including banks, hospitals, manufacturers, technology companies, utilities, and more. The easier observation is what isn't impacted. That's a short list. In other words, the threat is pervasive, and where the threat is so pervasive, the mitigation strategy is necessarily complex.

Several areas of improvement are needed in the development of public policy. Like the efforts to develop the atomic bomb and the race to the moon, the cyber defense initiative must be an extremely high priority. These vast initiatives required an integrated dedication by government and industry based upon the dimension of the threat. During World War II the necessity of developing the atomic bomb was based on the potential consequence of losing that conflict, which was an unacceptable outcome. While the cyber defense initiative is not equal in terms of impact, it is a model for winning the cyber wars. The race to the moon, begun during the John F. Kennedy administration, is a similar comparison. These ventures brought together the best minds, focusing vision and financial resources to prevail in times of great peril. Both World War II and the Cold War placed the United States and its allies at great risk of harm.

COLD WAR II: THE CYBER CHAPTER

Cold War II is taking shape. Its evolution, though developing at a rapid pace, is often hard to see. For years it was practically invisible. Cold War II will ultimately be the story of the cyber threat. Like forces mounting on the front in preparation for a massive offensive advance, the cyber threat is diversified, mobile, swift, and ultimately destructive and perhaps even disabling. What Cold War II lacks is visibility. In World War II the image of a foreign army invading domestic shores brought fear and uncertainty into the land, resulting in an unprecedented response throughout the nation that brought the United States and its allies to victory. In Cold War I, the Soviet satellite *Sputnik* and the parades of military might in Red Square signaled a new age, one of technological and military achievement for the Soviets and one of uncertainty for the United States and its allies. The space race was not just about the ability of a country to place into a low earth orbit a mechanical object with technological and communications capabilities. The larger statement was that the United States was behind in this race, and losing it held unacceptable strategic consequences. It represented a military threat, a threat to the economy and society, and to Western civilization.

Cold War II is at the early stage of this evolutionary trajectory. The cyber dimension is not just a tool of the economy. Ultimately, it is a weapon of vast offensive and defensive capability. The failure to develop it will result one day in a conflict in which there will be a winner and a loser. As in World War II and in Cold War I, the force of deterrence will decide victory. The atomic bomb and the space race signaled a power ultimately measurable in degrees of stabilization, economic growth, international trade, military restraint, and diplomatic relations.

The cyber dimension is a threat, yet it is also an opportunity. Left un-addressed, it is a threat that guarantees painful consequences in the form of expanded nation-state economic espionage, geopolitical realignment, retrogres-sive diplomacy, pervasive transnational criminal engagement, and even loss of military superiority. Anyone doubting the contribution to military superiority of the Internet need only consider advanced malware targeted at communications interruption, critical infrastructure disruption and disabling, intelligence collec-tion and enhanced analysis (Big Data), disinformation dissemination, and command and control interference and confusion.

The threat is clear, the opportunity less so. Right now, the strategy seems to be that industry is required to follow certain applicable regulations, which vary by circumstance and jurisdiction, though many industries have little or no regulatory requirements. Government pursues cyber security through many agencies and administrations. Critical infrastructure is a seeming hybrid of industry and government. These companies may sit in the private sector but must be responsive to the constantly changing threat condition. Companies want less regulation, government wants more of it. Consumers seem absorbed in the technology that enables mobility and social flourishing.

The difference between now and during World War II and Cold War I is one of perception and mission focus. World War II became an all-out effort to win the war, and the atomic energy program was the strategic focus to end the war in the Pacific. Nations thrive on multiple and sometimes disparate moving parts that seek to work synchronously in order to achieve a desired result: mission focus. This happened in World War II and in Cold War I's race to control space. A sense of destiny drove the nation. Destiny meant win or lose. Public policy reinforced the commitment to win. There was no middle ground. A middle ground was an indecisive result, leaving in question the outcome.

There is no sense of destiny associated with the cyber threat. There are several reasons for that. First is the misfire between government and industry, which can be seen in the government's timing and commitment level. The United States is quite likely behind China in the creation of a powerful and effective cyber force, making its position one characterized by the need to coordinate, accelerate, and surpass. It is easier for China, just as it was for the Soviet Union. Diversity of thought in communist regimes is subsidiary to the interests of the state. The cyber machine and mentality in China is not subject to voluntary participation, and funding is not subject to availability. In China, cyber is part of a strategy, an elemental piece of a larger strategy that permeates the national consciousness. Part military tactics, part intelligence collection, part economic espionage agent, and part economic expansion and global communications facilitation, all things digital are strands of a greater mission tied to China's interpretation of destiny.

That destiny won't work in the United States. The government in China may have made decisions pursuant to destiny, but its people have not. It's more complicated in the United States, and that makes cyber superiority even more difficult to achieve. The path to such a destiny in the United States will have to be paved with industry and the consent of the people. Public policy in the United States should reflect the will of the people, the will of industry, and the commitment of government to provide for the common defense of the best interests of the nation. Until such alignment shapes and sharpens the clarity of a cyber destiny, where the common defense of the future is an imperative, Cold War II will not result in favorable positioning.

Some argue that U.S. public policy reflects a cyber destiny. That's doubtful. It doesn't measure up to the examples of World War II and Cold War I. But why? What is the crucial difference between the race to build the atomic bomb or land on the moon ahead of the Soviets and the coming cyber threat? It's fear.

The nation feared an invasion of Japan and even the loss of the war to the Empire of Japan. Americans engaged in combat were dying daily. An invasion of Japan, it was estimated, could result in a million American casualties, even in victory. Fear of more loss of life than was necessary was a powerful incentive embraced by the government that ultimately was accepted by those whose loved ones could have perished in such an invasion. There was no shortage of fear in Cold War I. Visions of nuclear mushroom clouds, delivered by intercontinental ballistic missiles (ICBMs), filled the American consciousness. The race to space would establish at least technological parity, eventually resulting in a landing on the moon, a level of superiority translatable into military positioning and posing a retaliatory threat to an ambitious and acrimonious Soviet Union.

Today's cyber threat falls short of the fear factor of the past. No military invasion by flagged hostile powers is likely. No nuclear-tipped ICBMs trained on American targets pose a viable threat. Terrorists, transnational criminals, spies, and political and military use of the Internet have not yet aroused fear comparable to the historic fears of the past.

Almost by preapocalyptic definition, the cyber threat is not going to shape a public policy mandate. That will come after some grave event in the future. For now, the government may be expected to continue to work toward its stated goals as defined in the national cyber security agenda, including a program aimed at defending critical infrastructure. Law enforcement will continue its efforts in investigation and prosecution. The threat is considerable, funded by nation-states and criminal organizations that know no boundaries of geography or simple human decency.

In the absence of a quantifiable cyber destiny that meets the examples of decades past, the cyber threat will have to be met at the front gates of industry. Protecting the brand falls to those who own and manage the brand. This places a great burden on companies, which historically have not fared well in the face of the cyber threat. Largely misunderstood, the cyber threat has been a secondary concern by many in the private sector. Only recently has the boardroom begun to address the cyber threat within the context of the war on industry.

So as not to be misunderstood, the government is making strides and is taking action against the cyber threat. So is industry. That said, it is abundantly clear that the consolidated response to the cyber threat necessary to win the cyber war has not shaped public policy and has not sufficiently seeped into the psyche of an unprepared government and industry. In the final analysis, every company and every user has a responsibility in the cyber wars. But this is an uphill climb. While many companies are beginning to get the message, users don't think about security. There's no fear. Devices digital are part of work, part of pleasure and fun, part of the fabric of a mobile, digital life.

IS THERE A SILVER LINING IN AN ATTACK?

In the words of Winston Churchill, "A pessimist sees the difficulty in every opportunity; an optimist sees the opportunity in every difficulty." In the cyber defense, the country seems stuck somewhere in the middle. An opportunity does exist to advance the agenda of cyber security. It requires commitment. It requires cooperation, domestically and internationally. If there is a silver lining in the increasing number and severity of cyber attacks, it is that the result is visibility of the invisible. It is impossible not to be aware of the trends. In both houses of Congress, in the White House, in most any government around the world, in boardrooms throughout corporations large and small, for-profit and nonprofit, awareness of the predicament is growing.

There is opportunity in this difficulty. Politics have divided many efforts to ensure the integrity of the electrical grid, for example. In the United States, Democrats have favored more regulation, Republicans less regulation. Legislation at the federal level often reflects the great difficulties in passing new laws. The result is often watered-down legislation, based on intense disagreement and negotiation. Some state legislation can actually be stricter.

It was an attack on the electrical grid in California in the spring of 2013 that may hold the key to bipartisan efforts to protect the lifeblood of the country—electric power. In an act of sabotage, a Pacific Gas & Electric Corporation substation in Northern California was attacked, not over the Internet, but with tools that cut telecommunications cables and firearms that ripped into the substation. The severed AT&T fiber-optic lines disrupted phone and 911 service. According to media and government sources, more than 100 rounds hit the facility, disabling 17 of 20 large transformers.

Due to concern about the attacks and the vulnerabilities of this area of critical infrastructure, bipartisan support is surfacing for protection of these assets. A letter of February 7, 2014, from Senator Dianne Feinstein of California and several other senators to the chairman of the Federal Energy Regulatory Commission noted, "We are concerned that voluntary measures may not be sufficient to constitute a reasonable response to the risk of physical attack on the electricity system. While it appears that many utilities have a firm grasp on the problem, we simply do not know if there are substantial numbers of utilities or others that may have not taken adequate measures to protect against and minimize the harm from a physical attack."

Was this a dry run executed by foreign terrorists? Was it an extreme environmental group? The attack was sophisticated, and is under investigation by the FBI. Attacks against the electric grid and telecommunications infrastructure are a national security issue with immense implications where they succeed.

Voluntary measures are not enough to protect against physical or cyber attack. In fact, it is reasonable to forecast that future serious attacks against critical infrastructure are likely to be an integrated strike consisting of cyber and physical elements. Such an attack would create confusion and disruption of services, perhaps on a wide scale. Placing the political agenda behind the national security and safety interests of the nation is necessary. This is up to elected officials. There is no better time to pursue a bipartisan effort. The failure to act will have telling consequences.

Bipartisanship alone is not sufficient to meet the demand of the threat. Greater cooperation between government and industry is necessary. Yes, there are programs in place. And yes, there is communication. But there does not appear to be sufficient intelligence sharing about specific cyber attacks. It would seem reasonable that intelligence sharing would benefit everyone in the war against cyber attacks. Making this a requirement seems natural. But in the world of politics, what may seem unwaveringly logical is not always clear. Take, for example, a bill that should have passed to become law, a bill that would help the government and industry combat cyber attacks. The brief history of this bill is a lesson in how government, despite the best of intentions, is failing in some aspects of protection against cyber attacks.

But first, let it be stated here that those on the front lines of cyber defense, from law enforcement to the military and intelligence agencies, work hard in the defense against adversaries armed with computers and the Internet. Their work is often unrecognized, and their lives are often in jeopardy. Those they investigate are not beyond retribution. They are not the issue. But here's what is.

Government and industry are currently unable to share cyber threat information. Under Title XI of the National Security Act of 1947, it is illegal to share this information. Intelligence includes both foreign intelligence and counterintelligence. Officially, foreign intelligence means information regarding the "capabilities, intentions, or activities of foreign governments . . . foreign organizations, or foreign persons, or international terrorist activities."

Counterintelligence means the "information gathering, and activities conducted, to protect against espionage, or other intelligence activities, sabotage, or assassinations conducted by or on behalf of foreign governments . . . foreign organizations, or foreign persons, of international terrorist activities."

The range of information sources is broad, including the Office of the Director of National Intelligence, the Central Intelligence Agency, the National Security Agency, the Defense Intelligence Agency, the National Geospatial-Intelligence Agency, and the National Reconnaissance Office. Information also comes from the intelligence offices of the Federal Bureau of Investigation, the Department of State, the Department of Energy, the Department of the Treasury, the military branches, and elements of the Department of Homeland Security.

The National Security Act addresses "national intelligence" and "intelligence related to national security" and information involving "threats to the United States, its people, property, or interests." It also specifies information about "any other matter bearing on United States national or homeland security."

In the 112th Congress, in November 2011, a bipartisan bill, H.R. 3523, was introduced that would have amended the National Security Act of 1947 and its 2007 amendments to allow the government and industry to cooperate in the national cyber defense. Clearly, cyber attacks represent a threat to the "United States, its people, or interests." A bipartisan effort combating the escalating digital threat, H.R. 3523 was one of the few contemporary demonstrations of agreement between Republicans and Democrats. There was good cause for both sides of the political aisle to cooperate, and the bill was passed on April 26, 2012, by a vote of 248–168, including 42 votes by House Democrats.

Authored by Representative Mike Rogers (R-MI) and Representative Dutch Ruppersberger (D-MD), respectively the chairman and ranking member of the House Intelligence Committee, the bill would have allowed the U.S. intelligence community and private industry to share certain information about the complex array of cyber threats concentrated on the United States. Under strict rules and conditions, defined by the director of National Intelligence and monitored by Congress, industry and government would have been able to more effectively coordinate a defense against potentially devastating cyber attacks. Though the fact is hard to believe, it is currently illegal to share this information. It is worth noting that federal restrictions impeding information sharing between the FBI and the CIA contributed to the attacks of 9/11.

In order to have been eligible to receive intelligence, companies would have to have been able to demonstrate to the director of National Intelligence that classified information could be handled securely. The concept of the private sector possessing sensitive government information is not new. In fact, it is a long-held practice. Some 10,000 U.S. defense contractors have access to classified information, which requires special security protection. Has that record been perfect, free from abuse, from internal misuse and external acquisition? No. But the system does work. The fundamental framework is reliable, it is protective, and it can work to help defuse the cyber threat. However, H.R. 3523 died a quiet death in the Senate.

It was resurrected in February 2013 in the form of H.R. 624, the Cyber Intelligence Sharing and Protection Act. In late April that year it was passed in a bipartisan effort by the House in a vote of 288–127. The nonpartisan Congressional Research Service remarked of H.R. 624 that it "amends the National Security Act of 1947 to add provisions concerning cyber threat intelligence and information sharing." It would direct "the federal government to conduct cybersecurity activities to provide shared situational awareness enabling integrated operational actions to protect, prevent, mitigate, respond to, and recover from cyber incidents."

The bill also "defines 'shared situational awareness' as an environment where cyber threat information is shared in real time between all designated federal cyber operations centers to provide actionable information about all known cyber threats." H.R. 624 would direct "the DHS, Attorney General, Director of National Intelligence (DNI), and Department of Defense (DOD) to jointly establish and periodically review policies and procedures governing the receipt, retention, use, and disclosure of non-publicly available cyber threat information shared with the federal government."

The signing into law of H.R. 624 would enable a comprehensive effort to reduce the many risks associated with cyber attacks. It recognizes that such attacks are potentially devastating threats to the economy and to national security and that those threats represent rapidly evolving capabilities that can be difficult to identify, monitor, and mitigate. The bill recognizes that the cyber threat is an asymmetric, nontraditional national security and economic threat that requires the participation of industry and the government in order to be addressed. Sharing intelligence under tightly constructed rules is fundamental to addressing the cyber threat, arguably one of the most significant threats facing the nation. The United States has the capability to conduct this cyber defense program, it has the demonstrated need, but it lacks the purpose and immediacy to make this public policy. Unfortunately, there's little chance H.R. 624 or any successive legislation will pass in the Senate.

This condition is somewhat reminiscent of the days in this country leading up to December 7, 1941. Up until then, most polls showed that some 80 percent of the country had no appetite to fight Germany or Japan. Robert E. Sherwood, an American playwright and speechwriter for President Franklin D. Roosevelt, in the days leading up to that "day of infamy" observed that most Americans were more interested in the Army–Notre Dame football game. The surprise attack on Pearl Harbor changed everything.

It seems reasonable to suggest that the nation has failed to rally in support of a cyber war against its aggressors. The government knows the level and significance of the threat, much like it did before World War II. The people, however, in large measure, do not. Until there is enough pressure brought to bear on the political and legislative process, the will in Washington will remain in doubt. Public policy in support of a strong offensive and defensive cyber state reflects the interest level of the people and industry. Right now the focus is elsewhere, and there will be a price to pay for that.

Ideally, the war against the cyber threat would include most of the nations on the planet. A cyber crime in one country would be a cyber crime against all. But that is not the case, not really. There are levels of cooperation, yes. But it is not enough. Accept from government whatever intelligence and information is available. But don't depend on the government to solve the problem. Protecting the brand is the responsibility of every board of directors and every chief executive. Lobbying for better public policy will help. But until there is an attitudinal shift, perhaps brought about by a disabling cyber attack, circle the wagons around the brand and manage operational risk consistent with the threat level. Of course, establishing that threat level will require more guesswork until things change in Washington, D.C.

According to privacy attorney Ellen Giblin of the Ashcroft-Sullivan LLC law firm in Boston, Congress should "authorize the government to provide private companies with classified cyber threat information. Empower businesses to share threat information with each other and the government on a voluntary basis, and limit the liability for companies that share threat information."[2] None of the above will protect your brand and indemnify companies that suffer a cyber attack. But then again, the government is really not the vendor of the Internet. Financial institutions are looking to the government to indemnify them from attacks to online banking. Perhaps the government should tax or subject to fees each banking transaction on the

Internet to provide a central fund the banks can draw on to increase their security and make them whole after a cyber attack.

Failure to sign into law H.R. 624, or anything like it, is the digital equivalent of muffling the communications capability of the American Revolution's Minutemen, who served as an early warning and response system. Would the British attack by land or by sea? It is hard to fathom such an information and intelligence gulf between the colonial militia, the blacksmith, the farrier, the silversmith, and the lamp maker on April 18, 1775.

One thing we do know is that the next attacks are not likely to come by land or by sea, but by way of the Internet, ironically a communications system of last resort devised to prevent mutually assured destruction in a nuclear war. The real question is, how will we know if a cyber attack is about to happen? Perhaps the Cyber Intelligence Sharing and Protection Act should be renamed the Paul Revere Act of 2014. Maybe then it would pass with less resistance and become the law of the land. Everyone would be better off for it.

Thomas Paine said, "The instant formal government is abolished, society begins to act. A general association takes place, and common interest produces common security." Government is not likely to be abolished, but take Thomas Paine's observation under advisement. Think now. Act now. Society must act; nation-states and organized crime are already in motion.

 NOTES

1. U.S. Senate Hearing, "Safeguarding Our Nation's Secrets: Examining the Security Clearance Process," June 20, 2013, www.hsdl.org/?view&did=739426.
2. Conversation with Ellen Giblin, October 2013.

6

Four Trends Driving Cyber Breaches and Increasing Corporate Risk

Technological, Cultural, Economic, and Geopolitical Shifts

A ship is safe in harbor, but that's not what ships are for.

—*William G. T. Shedd*

A T A crowded restaurant in New York City a number of years ago, the maître d', a cultured, older man with silver hair and an air of confidence, recognized the couple, warmly acknowledged them, and heartily shook their hands as he walked them to a reserved table in a quiet corner of a busy room. He stayed for a few moments, telling them it was wonderful to see them again, and asked what they would like to drink. Before leaving the table, he again said how good it was to see them, and shook hands once more. After dinner the couple was preparing to leave. The restaurant by this time was quiet, the evening nearly over. As they pushed back from the table, the maître d' came and stood before them. With a broad smile and a sparkle in his eye, he said, "Perhaps you would like to have your watch back. It is a very fine piece." The diner looked at his wrist. There was no watch strapped to it, and a look of amusement crossed his face. "I had no idea," he said. "How?" Grinning, the maître d' said, "Don't feel badly. Nobody ever notices." Then, as if he were reflecting on another place and time, his smile faded, and he said soberly, "I wasn't always a waiter."

In that same way, mobile devices disappear. As noted previously, mobile devices are, well, mobile, and they're more apt to be lost or stolen.

 ## TECHNOLOGY TREND

Let's begin with the technology trend. Apple cofounder Steve Jobs once said at the unveiling of a new product, "An iPod, a phone, an Internet mobile communicator . . . these are *not* three separate devices! And we are calling it iPhone! Today Apple is going to reinvent the phone. And here it is." Technology is hot—but especially mobile technology. It is the future. The list of vendors offering devices and platforms and operating systems and applications is astounding. Mobile phones, smartphones, have been great contributors to redefining to a significant extent how work gets done and where work is done. The word has a nice ring, if you'll forgive the pun. Mention the word "mobile" to most people and it inspires a lot of notions. It means not being tied to an office or a desk. It means freedom, not from work but from the structure of work, perhaps. Mobility brings options and flexibility. It inspires lots of visions: keeping in touch while on vacation, making sure the house alarm is set, checking on the kids after school, conducting bank transactions.

Look at where investments in technology are focused and the answer is in social media and mobile technology. In large part, social media is being driven by mobile technology. There is the desire and demand to be virtual, to be mobile, flexible, fluid, responsive, connected continuously.

"Mobile devices have grown in acceptance by both private and corporate communities," says Danny Miller, system chief information security officer for the Texas A&M University System. "They occupy much of our time and minds. The wave of new smartphones, tablets, and e-book devices are creating an environment ripe for cross-platform malware to take root in our personal business operations such as online banking and at work with easy access to corporate asset information.

"The growing strength of malware will expose new sources of revenue to online criminals. These devices are running almost all of the same social and Web-based content that desktop devices have used for years. These newer, sleeker systems will only add to the onslaught of new vulnerabilities to these recently ported platforms. There will be crimeware threats for practically every mobile device or tablet OS platform and ported application."[1]

Mobility delivers a certain extension of freedom. More information is accessible across more platforms and from more locations than at any time in history. A number of researchers are forecasting significant growth over the next decade in mobile devices around the world. While forecasting out to 2025 is tricky, there are projections that 50 billion devices will be in the market by then. That's a huge number, but not irrational, and for this reason: When executives have been polled on the subject of how many mobile devices they carry, the average number is three or four—business laptop, business smartphone, business tablet, and personal cell or smartphone.

Looking at the developing markets around the globe, banks may be expected to provide mobile devices to populations who currently do not have a banking relationship, substantially increasing the number of customers and the number of mobile devices. Armed with a mobile device and electronic currency, banks will likely increase market breadth and depth. This initiative will drive mobile device growth.

In 2013 the United Nations reported that of the world's 7 billion inhabitants, 6 billion had a cell phone. However, only 4.5 billion had access to toilets or latrines. Mobile phone growth in Africa is linked to education. In fact, the majority of citizens in the country of Nigeria are linked to the mobile communications network. It is an essential part of the mission to provide education throughout the country. According to the United Nations, "Initiatives promoting mobile learning have already been spearheaded across a wide range of countries—including Mozambique, Pakistan, South Africa, Niger, Kenya, and Mongolia—where policies have already provided access to distance education in far-flung communities and improved literacy among girls and women."[2]

The UN research indicates that about "three out of four people have a mobile phone in Kenya and while only a third of Kenyans have access to the Internet, 99 per cent of this comes from mobile phones." Mobile technology has the ability to favorably impact developing nations in many ways, from improving education and health care, to helping to eradicate disease through awareness, to enhancing farming and agriculture. There's no doubt that mobile technology will benefit these efforts. Mobile technology is believed to be a powerful antipoverty tool. But it isn't that simple.

The history of computer and communications technology, including mobile technology, succinctly illustrates, for better or worse, the truism that the reach and expansion of technology is most often driven by perceptions and facts about lower costs, increased productivity, the use of technology as a force multiplier, expanded markets, enhanced presence, and so on. When enterprise-wide decisions are made, particularly among companies and in government and other organizations, security is not typically the driving consideration. It isn't security that makes the world go round, it's productivity. That's hard to argue against. On the other hand, without security, the risk of use increases, and the consequences can be significant.

Security has, it seems, always been in the backseat, and that's understandable if the mission is to generate revenue by selling hardware, software, and services. There's no argument in this corner. However, because technology's reach exceeds its grasp, in the form of security, there is the seemingly unstoppable problem of information compromise. The mobility factor doesn't increase security. In fact, the tide of security incidents will rise with the tide of mobile implementations.

The data backup service company Mozy came up with some interesting findings. According to Mozy, 80 percent of professionals work remotely at least some of the time, and more than two-thirds use memory sticks. A quarter of Americans lose their cell phones every year. Of 800,000 mobile devices lost or stolen in 2010, 97 percent were never recovered. The Ponemon Institute reports that 12,000 or so laptops are stolen or lost in airports in the United States every week. Is the number accurate? It doesn't matter. What does matter is that these devices are simply disappearing, whether lost or stolen. A significant number of them were targeted by criminals. And that is the point.

Executives and other employees are too often careless with laptops, especially in airports. Airports are public places, where many people feel unthreatened by criminal activity. There are usually police officers patrolling, and there are lots of people. Airports look and feel reasonably safe and secure.

When people feel reasonably safe and secure, their defense mechanisms slow down. People with laptops at the airport are thinking about things other than laptop theft. They are thinking about the upcoming business meeting at their next destination. Or maybe they're thinking about a promotion, a raise, getting back home to then head out on vacation. Perhaps thoughts of marriage, divorce, sports, kids, and any number of other things are at the forefront of their consciousness. That they are waiting to board the next flight does not seem to stimulate thoughts of security and awareness of surroundings.

 ## LOSS OF SITUATIONAL AWARENESS: DISTRACTION

One security executive who was fortunate enough to be assigned an aisle seat in the first-class cabin was using a BlackBerry while walking toward her seat. With too much to do and not enough time in which to do it, she was utilizing those precious moments to send out updates and respond to e-mail while walking. This has become something of a national techno pastime. Arriving at her seat, with a number of other passengers behind and in front of her and across the aisle, she needed to place her travel bag in the overhead bin above her assigned seat. Needing both hands to execute the maneuver, she innocently set the BlackBerry on the first-class seat. After placing the bag in the overhead bin, she reached down to retrieve her BlackBerry, but it was nowhere to be seen. She looked around quickly, even desperately. Somebody must have seen it. Did it fall off the seat and onto the floor? Could it fallen into the pouch on the back of the seat in front of her? Querying the nearby passengers and flight attendants was fruitless. No one admitted to having seen anything. Maybe someone saw something, maybe not. The result was the same.

People leave cell phones in taxicabs and other places all over the world, by the many hundreds of thousands, if not millions, every year. Many of these phones are smartphones and contain valuable data, often information regulated by various authorities. And many of these phones and tablets, even laptops and memory devices, are not password-protected. Steal the device and it's easily accessed. This is particularly true of many small and midsize companies, which may not have enforced information security policies, particularly in those companies—including some larger companies—that possess no regulated data or at least believe that they possess none.

It's easy to focus on the positive attributes associated with mobile technology. These devices are easy to carry, easy to conceal, easy to use, relatively inexpensive, increasingly powerful, and multifunctional, even indispensable. An entire generation is using computers that fit into the palm of a hand or, in the case of tablets, a small lightweight bag or sleeve; some of these people have probably seldom worked on a desktop machine.

It's not that desktop machines were secure. It is more that they were not as easily lost or stolen. So maybe they were more secure. People, or users, in the vernacular of the industry, remain the greatest threat to information integrity. A user could do less damage in the desktop era. Yes, information could be copied off of a hard drive. But it was hard to lose a desktop unless a thief broke into the office or home housing the unit and stole it.

Given that users are not well trained in security, and that data resides on increasingly small hardware platforms, the combination of carelessness and diminutive scale is a problem when it comes to protecting data. Just as the user may perceive device size and weight as a distinct operational advantage, especially when considering the power of these devices, a thief will appreciate their compactness and concealability. They are easy to steal in a swift and invisible strike.

 ## CULTURE

The culture at work and home and everywhere else in between is changing, in large measure because of technology. Mobility has helped define the culture of work and play. A generation ago, most people worked only at the place of work. Now people work everywhere, courtesy of mobile information and the devices that power accessibility. The line between work and home has faded, often to the point of obscurity. Conversely, the home has invaded the office. Workers may be checking e-mail at home at night, while at the office they may be participating in social networks, checking personal e-mail, and monitoring the kids' activities after school. What at one time was a line of distinction between these pursuits is now more of a fog of content. They aren't always clear, these lines of division, but it seems that this has become the accepted path to the future. Social protest has changed. Even in presidential elections, technology has helped define how to manage the process, how to reach voters, how to persuade the masses and influence public policy. Masses of political workers armed with smartphones, tablets, and the Internet are defining the future of political dynamics as they analyze data, interpret political dispositions, and calculate how to best influence outcomes.

Mobility also enables easier sharing of information, and this is a defining cultural issue. There is an expectation of sharing information, an expectation of information access. According to the report from the Office of the National Counterintelligence Executive discussed in Chapter 4, "The cultural shift involves the rise in the U.S. workforce of different expectations regarding work, privacy, and collaboration. Workers will tend to draw few distinctions between their home and work lives, and they will expect free access to any information they want—whether personal or professional—from any location."

So what are the concerns about wide-scale deployment of mobile devices? The organization Transparency International reports a lot of corruption in many of the nations where mobile device use will grow and where these devices will be distributed increasingly widely. From South Asia throughout most of the African continent, corruption is a major problem for which there does not seem to be a near-term solution. The intersection of corruption, mobile technology, and transnational organized crime represents a major risk, especially when taking into consideration serious security deficiencies and the emergence of unregulated electronic currencies. Laundering money generated through corruption and organized criminal interests is one expected outcome.

Think about it. Billions of people walking around with mobile devices. Laptops. Smartphones. Tablets. Surely this must fire the imagination of those with something to sell, as well as those with larceny on their minds—and revolution.

Picture thousands of people across the world sitting at desktop computers, engaged in social media. Could they participate in a distributed denial-of-service (DDoS) attack? Absolutely. Then consider the mobile variant. Could these same people create flash mobs and social protest on the fly? That's not as easy. But the ability to be mobile does make it possible. Using mobile communications allows for highly fluid and flexible gatherings, from a Benghazi-type terrorist action to a protest over just about anything.

Neither technology alone, nor mobility exclusively, defines the future of work, crime, social protest, terrorist strikes, and personal endeavors. The Office of the National Counterintelligence Executive has identified four trends that are defining the future. One of them is technology. In addition, economic, cultural, and geopolitical trends are contributing to rapid change.

 ## TECHNOLOGY IS A DOUBLE-EDGED SWORD

Let's start with the economic trend. The globe has become smaller, flatter, more accessible, as well as highly dependent on multinational trade. Technology drives the economy. The economy has also become infinitely more complex. Technology has become infinitely more complex, too, although it doesn't look that way to the average user. In fact, technology has become incredibly easy to use. That's why it is such a critical driver of the global economy: Everyone knows how to use it. That ease of use is a double-edged sword. Easy to use, easy to abuse. Nevertheless, technology is inseparable from the economic future. Certainly it is hard to imagine an economy without technology. It is becoming difficult to think about an economy that isn't stimulated by mobile devices, from mobile banking to mobile medicine to farming and agriculture. This is a mobile economy and the future may be expected to be even more mobile. Data travels with the workforce and the pleasure seekers of the planet.

Now consider the geopolitical trends. The U.S. government states that "a geopolitical shift will continue the globalization of economic activities and knowledge creation. National boundaries will deter economic espionage less than ever as more business is conducted from wherever workers can access the Internet. The globalization of the supply chain for new—and increasingly interconnected—IT products will offer more opportunities for malicious actors to compromise the integrity and security of these devices."[3] This is certainly the case with respect to mobile devices.

China and Russia remain the most crucial threats. The growing inter-relationships between companies in the United States and China illustrate this very well. China's economic reach is massive, and it has what many developed and developing nations need: money. Although there are indicators of financial stress in China, it remains a formidable player and will continue as such. Its financial strength ensures continued alignment with Iran, Pakistan, and others. It also means that as the cyber dimension evolves in the coming decades in emerging nations, such as those on the African continent, China will surely benefit, as it has with its cyber attack relationship with North Korea, which allows it plausible deniability.

Geopolitically, Russia also remains a threat. Of course, organized crime has been a continuing issue associated with Russia and much of Eastern Europe. But organized crime isn't the only problem. Many Russians with technical skills and experience live and work in the United States, and the Russian intelligence services are not beyond pressuring them to steal secrets as part of the country's economic espionage pursuits, a fact referenced by the Office of the National Counterintelligence Executive. More and more Russian companies are doing business in the United States. The employees of some of these firms are former Russian intelligence operatives.

Geopolitics also encompasses the subject of terrorism and cyber terrorism. While it may be politically disadvantageous for China or Russia to engage in a direct cyber offensive against the United States, that doesn't mean that neither country would benefit from such attacks. These attacks show where the United States' critical infrastructure is weak or strong, and what would have a major impact and what would have less of an impact. An attack of this kind would have the ability to disrupt critical supply chains and the distribution of power, among others.

Most of all, perhaps, it would announce to the world that the United States, or any other country targeted in an attack, has a soft underbelly. The massive credit card breaches of late 2013 and early 2014 are clear messages that this information is accessible, because it is vulnerable. Understanding vulnerability is essential. Taking advantage of it can be dangerous. But suppose that, say, North Korea or Iran, launching a cyber offensive against the West, is successful in leveraging identified vulnerabilities. That has value to China, and it has value to Russia. And although there are links between the nations, plausible deniability again surfaces. China or Russia could even look cooperative diplomatically by appearing to pressure the offending nation.

Maintaining a powerful cyber offensive capability is an element of geopolitical superiority and command. Subsidiary national relationships are necessary, and the cyber dimensions of such relationships are increasingly important.

"Cyber operations are very attractive to foreign intelligence organizations, non-state actors, criminals, and terrorists because they can be conducted relatively cheaply and easily and offer high returns with a low degree of risk," according to the Office of the National Counterintelligence Executive. "The risk of exposure is low because cyber operations can be carried out remotely and with a high degree of anonymity. In addition, cyber operations are comparatively inexpensive, and can be conducted rapidly. For all of these reasons, state and non-state actors are increasingly turning to the cyber domain to augment and bolster their respective intelligence activities against the United States in an effort to gain advantage."

Technology is shaping the development of all of these trends, and especially mobile technology, and it changes rapidly. Rapid change in technology is often referred to as Moore's law, and it is applicable here. Gordon E. Moore, a pioneer of Silicon Valley and a cofounder of semiconductor manufacturer Intel Corporation, predicted in 1965 that "the number of transistors incorporated in a chip will approximately double every 24 months." Says Intel Corporation, "Continuing Moore's Law means the rate of progress in the semiconductor industry will far surpass that of nearly all other industries.

The future of Moore's Law could deliver a magnitude of exponential capability increases, driving a fundamental shift in computing, networking, storage, and communication devices to handle the ever-growing digital content and Intel's vision of 15 billion intelligent, connected devices."[4] Although this exponential growth is expected to decline somewhat, to a doubling of growth every three years instead of two, that is still tremendous growth. But it seems the figure of 15 billion "intelligent, connected devices" may be a low estimate.

The growth of mobile technology and social media, as well as their impact on culture, economics, and geopolitics, is nothing short of remarkable. It enables productivity and commerce; that is undeniable. But it also enables the ability of potentially debilitating offensive attacks, widespread fraud, and politically expedient disinformation.

Technology will continue to advance. Culture will continue to evolve according to adoption trends in technology. Economics will continue to drive how technology is used and how culture adapts to change. Geopolitical influences will continue to divide nations as technology brings disparate societies together or tears them apart. That's the thing about technology: It is neither–or both–, consistently, friend nor foe. It is a tool of attack and defense. But the problem is that most users see their mobile devices and social networks as more friend than foe. That's why they share personal information so indiscriminately. And that's also why so many whose personal information is compromised are so surprised.

 NOTES

1. Author conversation with Danny Miller of the Texas A&M University System, January 2014.
2. "UN Agency to Use Mobile Phone Technology to Boost Literacy in Nigeria," UN News Centre, April 30, 2013, www.un.org/apps/news/story.asp?NewsID=44793.
3. National Counterintellgence Executive, 2009–2011.
4. Intel, "Moore's Law and Intel Innovation," www.intel.es/content/www/es/es/history/museum-gordon-moore-law.html.

CHAPTER SEVEN

Social Media and Digital Protest

No man is an island,

Entire of itself,

Every man is a piece of the continent,

A part of the main.

—*John Donne*

J UST AS no man is an island, neither is information technology an island, at least not anymore. Today information technology is a tool for the many, and its success is dependent on increasingly wide acceptance and fully engaged use. Information technology today isn't just a computer. It is computer-driven, yes. But it is much more than the ability to calculate and communicate. It is a revolutionary vehicle that is rapidly changing not only the way society communicates but the way it relates. Social media is shaping culture, religion, politics, economics, diplomacy, terrorism, and war. The flash-fire escalation of social media is a phenomenon of the Internet age. It is the ultimate congruence of hardware, software, services, and communications, fueled by low-cost, low-profile, multiuse physical devices that are literally in the hands of the young, the middle-aged, and the elderly alike. These devices pervade the home, the office, even the industrial workplace, as well as schools and universities.

Social media enables mass messaging and unprecedented influence capabilities, often at the drop of a tweet. Social media today is the ultimate example that no man is an island. Social media has created a powerful demonstration that the whole is in fact greater than the sum of its many, many parts. It has given voice to causes honorable and dishonorable, good and bad, legal and illegal, formal and informal, powerful and negligible. The voice of social media is often the loudest voice.

Social media is the magic powder of the era. It casts an incredibly wide, sometimes illusory, and enticing net. It is an elixir capable of bringing under its spell those near and far. It is perceived by many as a personal form of communication, an extension of self. Social media, it seems, has an intoxicating effect. There are those who use it indiscriminately, disclosing information without thinking twice. It has neither ethics nor morality, but it reflects those who use it, a sort of Narcissus reflection in a pond. And that is its greatest power, and its greatest weakness. Being careless in social media communications has gone viral.

Following is an example of how social media was used by hackers to profile a large number of banks. It started because bank employees didn't realize the importance of using social media with extreme caution. Much like in the use of e-mail, familiarity breeds not contempt but trust, or even passivity. Despite many warnings to the contrary, the employees (in one case, thousands of them) failed to exercise caution when using social media.

When using social media applications, the employees, while they did use their work e-mail addresses, didn't use their bank passwords. The banks' passwords were sufficiently complex, but the employees created different, easier, less complex passwords for social media. The problem was that hackers lay in wait for them, a sort of digital ambush. The hackers knew the employees would show up at the social media sites. Because the passwords used for the social media sites were easy to break, they were broken.

By breaking the passwords, the hackers were able to obtain a lot of useful information from bank employees as they continuously built profiles of the employees. They acquired the full names of employees, bank names, work addresses, names of colleagues, titles, photographs, reporting structures, and other information. The employees were being profiled in depth. Their profiles were found after a defensive search of hacker databases to see if bank employees were in fact being profiled. They were. But why?

These profiles are exploitable. The more information contained in the profile, the better for the hacker. Social media social engineering is on the rise. In fact, having access to this kind of profile data is a gold mine for anyone engaging in social engineering. Skilled social media social engineers are able to insinuate themselves into most any environment given enough information to work with. Phishing is a type of Internet identity crime, and spear-phishing is a variant. Phishing is typically an electronic communication sent to someone's e-mail address in an attempt to fool the recipient into responding and disclosing personal, confidential information. Often, the communication sent to the unsuspecting individual appears to come from a bank or sometimes even the Internal Revenue Service. The criminal perpetrating the hoax wants to fool the recipient into sending personal data back to the criminal. Phishing attacks usually are sent to many unsuspecting victims whose e-mail addresses appear on various lists. Spear-phishing is a more targeted approach, often aimed at higher net-worth individuals or who share certain other attributes in common. Maybe they belong to an association or other group. According to the FBI, "criminals need some inside information on their targets to convince them the e-mails are legitimate. They often obtain it by hacking into an organization's computer network [which is what happened in the previous case] or sometimes by combing through other websites, blogs, and social networking sites."

Phishing and spear-phishing attacks generate billions of dollars of revenue for criminal organizations and scam artists around the world. Bear in mind that the more information the dark side hackers have on employees in any company, the greater the risk of information compromise. That is why social media, used irresponsibly, elevates risk throughout the enterprise.

Anyone using a computer of any kind, from a desktop PC to a smartphone, knows that social media has become a dominant factor in the consumer as well as business marketplace. From selling real estate to marketing virtually every consumer product imaginable, social media is hot. It seems that most every company is engaged with social media. More than a decade ago, blogs, part of the social media experience, were becoming part of the landscape. They were a vehicle for ranting and venting, and companies were often the target. A company or product failed to meet expectations? Blog about it. A restaurant overcooked the steak? Blog about it and recount for everyone clicking onto the site about the quality of the food and service. The automobile manufacturer failed to stand by a warranty or the car broke down after a hundred miles? Blog about it—let everyone know.

Targeted companies railed about blogs, but blogging caught on. And now so has just about every other aspect of social media. Social media has gone mainstream. The Pew Research Center in 2003 estimated the universe of blogs to be some 4 million, growing to 8.8 million in 2004.[1] The Technorati research organization at that time forecast that 10,000 new blogs were coming online every day.[2] These numbers seems almost archaic, even quaint. Contrast those numbers with social media today. More than 1 billion mobile users visit Facebook every month.[3] So it seems that social media is here to stay.

 ## SOCIAL MEDIA: A TOOL FOR DISRUPTION, A MODEL FOR CHANGE

Social media is not all fun. It is a useful tool to those whose interests go beyond connecting professionally, sharing stories on everything from what's for dinner to birth and death announcements. It is also a very popular tool for professionals seeking to expand personal and professional horizons. There's very little that social media has not touched, including transnational organized crime and terrorist factions. And then there's the concept of social activism and social media. Think flash mobs.

Social media can bring large numbers of activists together, physically or technically. Both scenarios have happened. In the physical sense, social media can spread the word on where to go, when to be there, and what the cause of the day is going to be. People will assemble; people will protest. In the past, the World Trade Organization, the G-8, and the G-20 have been targeted. Protesters have been known to riot, pillage, plunder, shoot, and burn.

Throughout the Middle East and North Africa, civil upheaval has resulted in the overthrow of regimes, social unrest, military engagement, economic disruption, and many deaths of civilians and government representatives. The outcomes of what has become known as the Arab Spring, which erupted in Tunisia, Egypt, Morocco, Syria, Libya, Western Sahara, Djibouti, Sudan, Yemen, Saudi Arabia, the Palestinian Authority, Iraq, and elsewhere, are undecided. What is not in doubt is that social media plays a key role in enabling the coordination, assembly, awareness, and perhaps even funding of the social and cultural unrest unsettling the status quo. Social media is what makes these unfolding events unique.

As noted in Chapter 3, the Al Qaeda–sympathetic magazine *Inspire* is dependent on social media to attract and recruit adherents and to raise funds for terrorist engagement. This is social media and digital media shaping culture. And just as social media is shaping culture, social media is being used to commit criminal actions.

THE HACKER GROUP ANONYMOUS

The hacker group Anonymous has embraced social media and has used it to further its antibusiness agenda. Based on what has been garnered about Anonymous, its members are anti–intellectual property and trade secrets, anti-assets, and anti-ownership. This group of secretive, sometimes invisible hackers with great skill and global reach has adopted social media as an arm of its attacker profile. The myth with which Anonymous defines itself is that it is on the right side of justice. Not the law, but justice. The reality is that it is a loosely defined group of cyber thugs who make their own rules and enforce their vision of social justice on the rest of the world. Anonymous seems to believe that its members are the Billy Jack of social justice and social media. Of course, this is a perversion of reality. There is nothing virtuous about Anonymous.

For the uninitiated, *Billy Jack* was a 1971 feature film that came out in the midst of the Vietnam War and the height of the counterculture in America. The film is the story of a half-Navajo American Indian and Vietnam Green Beret combat veteran. He becomes a vigilante in defending the hippie-esque Freedom School against the local townspeople, who are headed by a wealthy rancher-villain. The rancher-villain and his gang of thugs represent the status quo, the local power base. They are the establishment and they feel threatened by change. The Freedom School represents that change. Billy Jack is the defender of the school. He is a tough guy, played by the actor Tom Laughlin. Trained in martial arts, Billy Jack can kill with his hands and feet. He is the ultimate vigilante: virtuous and on the side of right.

The story line is this. One day, a busload of students, including Navajo from the Freedom School, arrive in town for ice cream. Billy Jack protects the children from abuse and harassment by the rancher-villain's son and his friend. A punch here, a kick there, and the bad guys are down and out for the count. But outside, the rancher-villain and his followers await Billy Jack. The rancher-villain arrives and squares off with Billy Jack. He is pompous, wealthy, seemingly in control of his universe. He's overweight, middle-aged. He rules his world, or so he thinks. Billy Jack is surrounded. The villain-rancher says with a condescending smirk to Billy Jack, "Big Indian chief, so special, so above the law. You think can do just as you please."

Then, in one of the more poignant moments in the film, Billy Jack explains what is going to happen next. Realizing that there is no way out of his predicament, he says, "You know what I'm going to do . . . just for the hell of it. I'm going to take this right foot, and I'm going to whop you on that side of your face," pointing to the right side of the villain-rancher's head. "And you know something—there's not a damn thing you're gonna be able to do about it." Then the villain-rancher is down.

Anonymous believes it is the Billy Jack of the Internet and that there isn't much global law enforcement can do to stop it, despite the fact that Anonymous hackers were arrested in 2013 for attacks against a variety of targets, including organizations supportive of intellectual property ownership. There's one key difference, though, between Anonymous and the film character. The film character possesses the value of tolerance, a value unknown to Anonymous. Anonymous wants the world to reflect its vision of what is right, and falling outside that narrow definition subjects anyone to the scrutiny of Anonymous, and possibly targeting by the group.

Anonymous Is an "Anti" Outfit of Malcontents

Anonymous is anticopyright, anti–intellectual property, anti–trade secret, anti-anything it deems as inappropriate or unfair: Information is for sharing, not owning. This appears to be its credo. Anyone who wants information should be able to have free and unrestricted access to it. Anonymous is anti–villain rancher, antiestablishment. It is, in its own frame of reference, the freedom fighter of the Internet and the Web. Anonymous seems to think of itself as the Billy Jack of the virtual world. Of course, it isn't. The Anonymous vision of itself is an illusion. At its best, it is a nuisance, at its worst, a criminal enterprise. Unlike the fictional movie hero, members of Anonymous hide behind the secrecy and invisibility of the Internet. They are confrontational only to the extent that they believe that they are invincible and cannot be caught, but that assumption is proving to be incorrect as law enforcement continues to unravel the identities of Anonymous members.

Social media is clearly changing business, just as it has enabled Anonymous, taking it to a higher level of influence, action, and impact. It is changing how people socialize, communicate, even mingle, date, and marry. Some believe in the positive power of social media, while others believe it trivializes relationships and replaces relationship integrity with the shell of a relationship. Both camps are probably right. But the impact of social media is undeniable. The case for Anonymous is interesting in that, unlike the

Arab Spring, traditional social protest designed to orchestrate assembly, the goal of this loosely held organization is to assemble online to conduct disruptive attacks against specified corporate targets. Anonymous taking on the rights associated with intellectual property is telling.

Anonymous is a loosely affiliated network of social activists and hackers. Some are very technically proficient. They understand the intricacies of hardware, software, information systems, information security, and how to defeat security and availability of information. The members of Anonymous, which dates back to 2003, are essentially hackers with a cause. They are both hackers and social activists and are fond of referring to themselves, as others also refer to them, as "hacktivists." While Anonymous is, well, anonymous, many of its members are known to law enforcement around the world and many have been arrested. The law enforcement community has become much more technically sophisticated and has gained a great deal of experience in combating cyber crime, and it is increasingly difficult to be invisible on the Internet. Not that it can't be done, but it is increasingly difficult to hide behind the veil of anonymity.

Anonymous in the past has attacked a diverse range of targets, including the governments of the United States, Israel, Uganda, Tunisia, and other countries. It has attacked legitimate corporations, and supported the widely publicized Occupy movement, a social protest against economic and political inequality. It also supported WikiLeaks, which was involved in the leaking of classified security information supplied by U.S. Army private first class Bradley Manning. Yet Anonymous has also focused its considerable prowess on targeting child pornography sites. The group has its own code of social justice and is empowered by social media.

A scan of the Web shows that while Anonymous members may be cloaked in secrecy, its profile is not. The group has an international reputation. Some refer to Anonymous as freedom fighters. Others call them cyber terrorists. Whether digital Robin Hoods or cyber criminals, the organization has been breaking numerous U.S. domestic and international laws. The fundamental philosophy of Anonymous is at odds with most governments and industry, so it should come as no surprise that its members are coming under more scrutiny by law enforcement.

Although Anonymous was believed to have become relatively quiet by 2009, after its attack on film actor Tom Cruise and the Church of Scientology, it reemerged. The group operates from bases in a number of countries, using computers and Internet connectivity that is difficult to associate with specific members. The FBI has described Anonymous as a loose affiliation of individuals with no defined leadership or membership. "In practice, the label

Anonymous is the banner under which individuals or groups commit actions, including intrusions into computer systems." Anonymous has made some strategic errors. One such error may have been to target law enforcement in its cyber attacks, which could be a powerful incentive for law enforcement in turn to target Anonymous.

In Reckless Move, Anonymous Targeted Law Enforcement

In 2012, the FBI arrested a 21-year-old man believed to be associated with Anonymous. According to the U.S. federal complaint, filed in the District of Utah, the defendant has links to a group associated with the hacker-activist network. The indictment alleges that the defendant hacked into protected computers without authorization on two occasions in January 2012 and intentionally caused damage to servers hosting web sites for two Utah law enforcement agencies. The first intrusion took place on January 19, 2012, and involved a server hosting a web site for the Utah Chiefs of Police Association. The second count alleges a similar attack on January 31, 2012, on the server hosting the Salt Lake City Police Department web site. FBI agents in the case traced the IP addresses used in the attacks to the defendant.

Anonymous has for many years been terrorizing companies and governments, including law enforcement. In 2013, Anonymous Indonesia is believed to have broken into more than 170 Australian web sites because these mostly small businesses and organizations had simply cooperated with U.S. intelligence agencies, a no-no among the antiestablishment members of this hacker group. Ongoing investigations across multiple jurisdictions, and arrests and prosecutions of some of its members, have yielded information about Anonymous's identities. Whether acting independently as arbiters of what they believe to be right, or even selling their services to nation-states and other groups, members of the group are behind many cyber attacks and possess a great deal of influence.

The behaviors of members of Anonymous are as interesting as they are illegal. They often envision themselves as cyber superheroes fighting evil and injustice. But their superpowers are not derived from comic book fantasies. Their superpowers come from computer wizardry. While not all hackers have this level of sophistication, some do, and that's all that it takes to do damage. These are the leaders. This is where social media and social protest converge with the interests of Anonymous, and with others who use protest as a social voice of opposition.

Several trends have converged that have allowed Anonymous to lead and others to follow, creating a dangerous cyber weapon. The low cost of technology, the almost unimaginable growth of mobile devices around the world, omnipresent social media, continuous availability, and the variable degree of anonymity offered by the Internet have enabled a powerful form of protest and digital assembly.

The Web is a massive marketplace and a criminal's dream. In the case of Anonymous, the organization has confused criminal conduct with social protest. The Web has become a social rallying point, and Anonymous has taken advantage of the condition. The digital flash mob has been born, and Anonymous has used it in an attack on industry, not for any peaceable assembly.

Anonymous has used social media to conduct a form of cyber attack known as a distributed denial-of-service attack (DDoS). These are simply attacks that flood a particular Web address with so much traffic that the address becomes clogged to the point that it is unresponsive. It's New York City at rush hour, complicated by a massive parade and garbage and transit strikes, when every resident of Manhattan is trying to get to New Jersey to respond to an offer of free real estate. Everything stops. Nothing moves.

In a DDoS attack, many people and devices flood a specified Web address, causing that address to become dead in the water, so to speak. The trick is to get as many devices as possible on the offensive against the site. This is where social media and recruitment weigh in. This is the place where leaders come to inspire, recruit, and direct digital adherents.

This isn't the only DDoS attack strategy, but it is effective and works well—until it doesn't. This was the case in the late 2013 arrests of 13 members of Anonymous, all of whom were charged in a grand jury indictment by the Department of Justice in the Eastern District of Virginia. The federal indictment is payback for, well, Operation Payback, an online conspiracy between the 13 defendants and others in what the indictment describes as "coordinated series of cyber-attacks against victims."

Anonymous members and their online participating sympathizers, as well as their coconspirators, believe that all information should be free. It's that simple. Free information for the asking—or the taking. It wouldn't matter who created the music, the movie, the literature, the news, the science, the technology, the invention, the concept. Everything should be free, available to anyone, anytime. According to the indictment, Anonymous, through Operation Payback, "targeted victims worldwide, including governmental entities, trade associations, individuals, law firms, and financial institutions."

Anonymous: Making All Information Free for All

Those organizations became targets because Anonymous claimed that the institutions are opposed to the "stated philosophy of making all information free for all, including information protected by copyright law or national security considerations." This is the opposite of what Anonymous believes.

Operation Payback hit a wide range of entities, but all the victims shared a connection: a connection to restricted information that had financial value. Anonymous tapped into a vein of common sentiment among its followers. Those followers believed, as Anonymous did, that information had value, and that no one had the right to own and benefit from that ownership. The victims of its attacks possessed no rights with respect to their own information or to charge fees for the use of the information. Some of the Anonymous victims were reasonably high-profile organizations, though not all were. Targeted organizations included the Recording Industry Association of America, the Motion Picture Association of America, the U.S. Copyright Office of the Library of Congress, Visa, MasterCard, and Bank of America.

Operation Payback had a life span of about a year, beginning on or about September 16, 2010. The indictment charges that Anonymous launched a "series of cyber-attacks against victim websites by flooding those websites with a huge volume of irrelevant Internet traffic with the intent to make the resources on the website unavailable to customers and users of those websites." The weapon of choice in this protracted cyber offensive was a free online testing tool known as Low Orbit Ion Cannon (LOIC), which is used legitimately to stress test computer networks. What Anonymous did was to publicize its pending attacks and recruit as many followers as it could, getting its politically charged adherents around the world to simultaneously fire LOIC tools at selected targets, rendering the victim web sites temporarily unavailable.

In its recruitment efforts, Anonymous made decisions about which targets to strike and then publicized the intended targets and their IP addresses. Anonymous then announced the dates, times, and any other required instructions needed to bring its followers in on the coordinated attacks. They communicated to their followers the attack tool of choice, LOIC, and continuously recruited for the events. They recruited using Web bulletin boards, social media sites, and dedicated online chat rooms known as Internet relay channels, or IRCs.

"We target the bastard group that has thus far led the charge against our websites, like the Pirate Bay," Anonymous posted in an online message. "We target MPAA.ORG," the group wrote about the Motion Picture Association of America, which was targeted in this case because of the Pirate Bay, the Anonymous-supported file-sharing web site based in Sweden that was dedicated to illegally downloading copyrighted information. MPAA shut down the Pirate Bay, infuriating Anonymous and prompting the retaliatory measure.

In an illustration of its reach and influence, Anonymous circulated an online flier that noted the MPAA IP address as it recruited its followers. Anonymous instructed, "The IP is designated at [deleted], and our firing time remains THE SAME." Anonymous gave directions on how its followers should proceed. "Install the LOIC linked above into any directory you choose, load it up and set the target IP to [deleted] port 80 Method will be TCP, threads set to 10+, with a message of 'Payback is a bitch . . . ' Everything else must be left blank. Once you have the target locked, DO NOT FIRE. REPEAT: DO NOT FIRE!" The electronic instruction continued, "This will be a calm, coordinated display of blood. We will not be merciful. We will not be newfags. The first wave will be firing in: ONE DAY: 09/17/2010 9pm EASTERN. When it comes time to fire, ignore all warning messages. They mean nothing. Keep firing."

Anonymous was monitoring the MPAA attack progress as if it were following a military assault. One member of the group during the attack noticed that MPAA.org had moved to another IP address as a defense against the continuing attack. In a plea for more help from the attackers, the Anonymous member posted online the message, "Need thread guys! MPAA.org is back! they have a new IP . . . someone took notice." Anonymous then stated that on the following day there would be an attack on the Recording Industry Association of America.

In Pursuit of the Anonymous Definition of Civil Liberties

A member of Anonymous recently said that the "guiding principles behind it are positive change, the restoration and preservation of liberty and freedom and individual rights." This is a difficult position for Anonymous because it seems inconsistent. Do liberty, freedom, and individual rights, which it says it seeks to protect, allow creators of information to prosper from their efforts? Apparently not. Anonymous gets to name its principles but there is great inconsistency in its logic.

Fourteen other Anonymous members have been arrested in Ankara, Turkey, for commission of cyber crimes in numerous cities throughout that country. Their attacks were against government web sites.

The FBI has stated that Anonymous has been broken. Maybe, but that is not likely. Every time one Anonymous member is arrested, another moves in line to assume the vacated position. Anonymous has a big bench and there seems to be no shortage of those willing to fill its seats. But the FBI made a very good point: Anonymous members eventually slip up. They make a mistake, which enables law enforcement to make arrests. In the case of the 13 arrests in association with the attacks against MPAA and others, one of the Anonymous members participated in an attack from his home computer, which led the FBI to his home address. Simply put, he got lazy.

Anonymous and other groups like it are not on the way out. In fact, they are increasingly dangerous because of their access to increasingly powerful low-cost technology and to large numbers of followers through social media, which is growing rapidly. While it is true that law enforcement is making significant gains, groups like Anonymous are here to stay. Their members may change, their tactics may evolve over time given changes in technology, but these rogue hacker groups remain a significant threat to business and governments around the world. The actions of Anonymous that come directly from its members make it clear that it is a continuing threat. Failure to defend against attackers of this type will result in loss. Operational risk management and information security organizations must protect their environment and their intellectual property and other proprietary information.

Technology and anonymity have given a voice and a weapon to those who in previous generations have not had that voice and weapon. Anonymous and its members do not appear to be in it for the money. In part, that is what makes them dangerous. They are driven and inspired by ideology. They get to make their own rules and their own rules of engagement. For Anonymous, there is power in righteousness, and they believe they are right and righteous. While they may come from many backgrounds, they share in common a goal that is antithetical to the fundamental principles of business.

During the Cold War between the United States and the Soviet Union, there were some American citizens, including those in the military and in the defense industry, who betrayed their country and worked for the Soviet Union. While some were traitors for money, many more were inspired by ideology. Those were the dangerous ones. Their principles, regardless how skewed and inconsistent with any logic, were the guiding light of their actions.

Anonymous members share this attribute, and that is what empowers them. It would be a monumental mistake to underestimate the range, influence, and impact of their actions. Social media has for Anonymous and groups like them created a vast network of followers, who may or may not agree with every tenet of the principles of Anonymous. But the careful targeting of specific victims, based on very specific principles, such as property ownership and other values adopted by much of the world, have enabled Anonymous to bring together a formidable attack strategy.

ANARCHAOS: IN THE IMAGE OF ANONYMOUS

Another hacker group appearing in the headlines in 2013: Anarchaos, a portmanteau of "anarchists" and "chaos." In May 2013 one of its members pleaded guilty to U.S. federal hacking charges. The hacker admitted to forcibly breaking into the computer systems of Stratfor, an intelligence company that has government and private-sector clients, in 2011. He also admitted to breaking into FBI training center computers. Breaking into systems belonging to law enforcement and companies working with law enforcement is something of a digital death wish. But it is also a signal of arrogance, one of the trademarks of professional hackers.

The judge in the Anarchaos case in U.S. district court in New York City didn't accept the hacker's defense. The defense? He said his actions represented "a new form of protest." Good for the judge. There are a number of ways to protest using digital technology: Developing a web site dedicated to the advocacy of the cause, creating a blog or writing in someone else's blog, or expressing opinions on social media web sites around the world are all options. Twitter is often used for advocacy. It's lawful in the United States to assemble under most conditions, and it's lawful to coordinate and stimulate assembly using the Internet. This is all a legitimate form of protest. But hacking into another's computer system is not a legitimate form of protest. It is breaking and entering.

Suppose someone breaks into a house. The homeowner, the victim, holds an opinion antithetical to the intruder. The intruder plots and plans, coming up with a method to override the security of the locks securing doors and windows. It's the security system. Once inside, the intruder searches for documents outlining the target's positions, strategy, goals, and so on. He changes the documents, or maybe burns them. Regardless, the integrity of the home and possessions is now compromised. The intruder may destroy documents or maybe deface the walls by painting symbols on them, or maybe sinks and tubs are filled to capacity and then overflow, ruining floors, perhaps destabilizing the electrical system. Perhaps the intruder barricades himself inside the structure, not allowing anyone access, but invites certain people to come over and occupy the house with him. This is basically what some hackers do in the digital world. While most people would object to anyone controlling or accessing anyone's personal home or business without permission, because it happens in the virtual world there is not as much outrage. Hackers are sometimes given a pass by society. "They're expressing themselves," some say in defense. "It's just the Internet." "They're just kids." "People have the right to speak their mind."

Hackers often believe that their rights transcend the rights of others. Clearly that is the case with the members of Anonymous and Anarchaos. From the earliest age of computer use by the masses, certain individuals who possess computing skills for perhaps the first time in their lives feel a sense of empowerment. Perhaps they didn't feel that way in school. Maybe they had dead-end jobs. This was their path to another world, one in which they evolved in a way different from their more digitally challenged peers.

Some went on to work for the government, some joined the corporate workforce. Some moved to the dark side, where Anonymous lives. Are its members narcissists? Are they frustrated computer nerds who can, so they do? The motives of Anonymous are not as important as its actions. Everyone is entitled to an opinion. Even facts are often fluid, based upon interpretation and perception. But the actions of Anonymous, and other groups similar to it, are outside the legal framework of most nations. It is also true that the use and manipulation of social media is going to increase, and much of the manipulation will be by groups such as Anonymous, other hacker groups, and also by terrorists seeking recruits, capital, internal messaging, and the ability to assemble on demand.

The ability to use social media to foment support for protests and boycotts against virtually any enterprise, government or industry, is increasingly an operational risk. It will also become an even more compelling and effective attack vector for Anonymous and those sympathetic to its cause as social media use and mobile device proliferation continue.

 NOTES

1. Pew Research Center, www.pewresearch.org.
2. Technorati, www.technorati.com.
3. *PC Magazine*, Spring, vol. 24, 2014.

PART III

Protecting the Brand

*Actions Executive Management
Must Take to Reduce
Cyber Risk*

CHAPTER EIGHT

Managing the Brand When the Worst Occurs

A crisis unmasks everyone.

—*Mason Cooley, professor, aphorist*

CHANCES ARE, if it hasn't yet happened, it will. Maybe a breach has occurred and it just hasn't been uncovered; this is as common as it is disturbing. Sometimes a worst-case scenario doesn't look that way at first. It's sort of like looking at a spitting cobra through a window only to discover too late that one of the panes is missing. The experience may be interesting, terrifying, even mesmerizing. And then you feel the sting, followed by immense pain.

This chapter is intended to provide a general outline for responding to a cyber breach. It is not a specific, defined breach response to every situation. Not all companies are the same, and not all breach events are the same. Attacks are launched against different targets by different attackers in various countries. Even motive from one attack to the next varies, sometimes greatly. Enterprise preparedness is extremely variable, ranging from very good to virtually nonexistent. Preparedness is interpreted differently. Some organizations don't see much risk, others become consumed by it. Some companies strive to be compliant with industry guidelines and meet a variety of government regulations, while others remain unaware of the regulations or intolerant of them. Being prepared means different things to different people. In the absence of specified recommendations, interpretations are derived based on an organization's risk tolerance. The real problem with determining risk tolerance is that many entities measure that degree of tolerance differently. Basically, there's trouble ahead.

The best advice is this: Prepare for it. Don't wait for the breach to occur to take action. As Mason Cooley remarked, a crisis really will unmask everyone. Some who become unmasked will show that they are not in the least prepared. Others will demonstrate competence and preparation. The unprepared will not expect a breach. The prepared, even though they may be surprised when it comes, will at least not believe that it was unexpected. When a company is unmasked as unready, it truly is a crisis, because its brand is on the line. While many may to be blame, a few will come into the crosshairs as the investigation evolves. A company unmasked and found to be incompetent will have a hard time living down the reputation it will have developed. A company unmasked and found to be ready for the crisis will stand a far greater chance of overcoming it.

The common denominator between the two kinds of companies is that both are likely to suffer at least one breach, and both will be subject to intense scrutiny in the examinations that arise from the breaches, whether from one or more federal, state, and foreign country regulators; opposing legal counsel; insurers; business partners; investors; and corporate contract customers.

When a breach of security or of actual data occurs, it is necessary not to lose time. Time is, as they say, of the essence. But it is equally important not to act without thinking about the problem at hand. Some managers think and act well under pressure. Others do not. A breach of information can get complicated quite rapidly, and having a basic structure to follow is important. Many companies have developed incident response and data breach plans. It's always important to get legal buy-in on such plans of response and action.

Assume that every breach will have the capability to disrupt company operations. Also assume that the breach will become public. While some companies are able to avoid reporting a breach legitimately, others will hide it. But very few companies that experience a breach of regulated data will be able to avoid reporting it in every jurisdiction. Companies that have legally been able to avoid reporting breaches in the United States have been forced to report them in other countries. This can be very costly and painful. Even companies that do not have to report a breach, perhaps because no regulated data was involved, may find that the brand is compromised. Word gets out through a number of channels. Maybe a former employee who knows about the breach mentions it after going to work for a competitor. Or maybe that former employee was not restricted from mentioning the breach because management assumed the employee didn't know about it. Maybe the employee who goes to another employer was involved in or responsible for the breach. This has certainly happened on a number of occasions. The employee either made a mistake, which contributed to the breach, or there was a malicious act that led to the breach. This is not uncommon.

In the case of an employee who makes a mistake, it can be forgiven, and additional training may be able to prevent that employee from committing the same mistake twice. Awareness of any deficiencies that led to that administrative error can be increased. It is feasible that under the term of lessons learned, a relatively minor breach can contribute to the prevention of a major breach at a later date. But in the case of the malicious act, the employee is usually terminated. Here's a problem, though. These employees are often not arrested and criminally prosecuted. The reason is clear: Management and the board believe that a public airing of the breach in the form of a criminal prosecution will bring an extraordinary level of awareness into the public record. While such matters may be handled adequately to manage the brand reputation, many companies still shy away from going public.

Unfortunately, even in the event of a malicious action leading to a serious breach and compromise, when the employee is terminated, that individual is likely to go to work at another employer. Because there is no criminal record on file, the worker can be employed by another company. The event won't show up on a background investigation either, unless the investigative process is rigorous—and most definitely are not.

Unless strict precautions are taken to prevent disclosure, word will get out. From there, it is a short jump to social media and the press. This can become an uncontrolled brand management nightmare.

There's really only one way to manage this kind of crisis. Anticipate what is going to be needed and have a plan. Clearly, companies have varying requirements, and every company is somewhat different. Industry sector is a differentiation, as is size of company, geographic distribution, regulatory and legal jurisdiction, and other factors. But there are consistencies among companies, too. For the purpose of this chapter, assume a company based in the United States.

Always bring in an external security and forensics firm. A lot of companies think they can best handle a breach internally, but this is almost never the case. And then there's the chance that a member of the team may be involved in the breach. Having a forensics firm on call enables independent judgment, which will prove valuable when dealing with regulators and opposing legal counsel.

 BE PREPARED

Bear in mind that a typical breach investigation will be conducted in five distinct but interconnected phases. These phases are: (1) initiation; (2) forensic evidence capture; (3) Web and behavioral analytics; (4) risk impact analysis; and (5) reporting to constituent groups, internal and external.

1. Initiation

- Establish attorney-client privilege prior to the event and the breach investigation, for oral and written communication, including e-mail, Web postings, and other forums as appropriate to disclosure. Determine, with the assistance of legal counsel, what to include in written communications. Discuss the issue with the general counsel or other legal counsel with the authority to approve the activity. Not all companies have an in-house legal counsel. If there is no internal general counsel, discuss the issue with the appropriate external legal counsel. Make certain the legal counsel has experience in data breach management, data protection, privacy, and regulatory compliance, as well as third-party vendor management. This can be an issue for smaller companies with no in-house counsel. The smaller firms may rely upon the advice and counsel of the attorney that has been used for a wide variety of other issues, and this is one area in which expertise and experience are critical to success. Consider these options for the establishment of attorney-client privilege, as appropriate to prevailing conditions:
  - Use of in-house counsel
  - Use of external counsel
  - Use of combination of in-house and external counsel as appropriate
- Establish a breach investigation management team. Conditions may vary, but in general include members with the following roles and responsibilities:
  - **General counsel** or other legal representative, as noted in the prior section.
  - **Executive sponsor**, if not the legal representative. However, since the legal representative will play a critical role, this is a good option.

This is especially true in the event of a breach involving regulated personal information, including medical and financial information.

■ **External legal counsel**, as appropriate to individual client circumstances. External legal counsel may play a role in the team under certain circumstances. If the in-house legal officer does not have the specific experience and background, it may be advantageous to have an external lawyer with such experience on the team.

■ **Internal security**. This may be the chief information security officer (CISO) or, in larger companies, the CISO and the chief security officer (CSO). The CISO/CSO should not necessarily lead the investigation but should play a key role. The reason that the CISO/CSO should not have the lead role is that whatever the outcome, there is going to be a legal consequence. It may be a civil or even a criminal matter. It may be a regulatory issue. That is why it is so important to have the general counsel or an equivalent run the investigation. In some companies, this is behind the practice of having the CISO or CSO report to the top legal officer of the company.

■ **Internal IT infrastructure**. The breach took place within the infrastructure, either technically or operationally. Technically, it could have happened over the network. Operationally, it could have been a stolen computer or other device.

■ **Human resources**. Insiders are often the cause or the source of the breach, so that makes it a human resources problem. HR's level of involvement will be determined by whether or not the employee(s) involved was engaged in a malicious act. HR may also be asked to participate in a "lessons learned" awareness program as part of an enhanced information risk management program. They may also need to validate the existence of the current awareness program, in cooperation with the CISO or CSO.

■ **Corporate communications**. This member or team can help communicate both internally as well as to the media should that be an outcome of the investigation. The involvement of the member or team from the outset will help shape the message and the outcome.

■ **Privacy or regulatory compliance**, as appropriate. The problem is that not every company has a privacy or compliance officer. One reason is that companies that do not manage personal information are often under the mistaken notion that privacy is applicable only to personal information. Business proprietary information is equally valuable. Every company, regardless of size and business, should assign someone to watch over the privacy of information.

- ▪ **Risk management.** Not all companies have a chief risk officer (CRO), but some do. That risk officer should always be involved and work closely with the legal officer on all matters regarding the breach. Where there is a CRO, that individual should participate in the board-level briefings.
- ▪ Establish chain of custody requirements consistent with U.S. Department of Justice guidelines. There's a very real possibility that the imaged drives of the company's computers will contain evidence that will be presented in court or to regulators, and even insurers and business partners. Demonstrating that strict procedures were followed can be convincing that the company, despite a breach, is handling the predicament efficiently and skillfully.
- ▪ Establish internal communication standards and protocols:
  - ▪ Assign a point person of contact for external communications with consultants, advisers, and so on. Sometimes this can be a communications team member, even a security team member. Typically, though, it is the legal officer assigned to the case.
  - ▪ Assign a point person for communicating with the audit and risk committee of the board of directors. Again, this is often the legal officer, but the legal officer may want to seek the advice and counsel of others on the breach investigation team. There are two kinds of meetings with the board. One is a meeting, either formally or informally, with the head of the risk committee. The other is a meeting with the full board.
  - ▪ Establish a frequency and method of progress communication with various constituent groups. The core of the group—legal, security, risk, IT, and several others—may need to meet periodically throughout the day in the early stages of the breach because conditions may fluctuate and things may change rapidly. Flexibility is the key to staying on top of a fast-changing environment. The full team should meet twice daily at first for status condition, in the morning and then at the end of the day.
  - ▪ Establish encryption standards for written communications, including e-mail and other documentation. This is important, especially when it is uncertain whether the breach is still under way and the extent of penetration and compromise is unknown.
  - ▪ Depending on circumstances, contain breach information to the breach management team.
  - ▪ Advise employees at the appropriate time, but in the interim try to contain the information to the smallest circle possible. During many

breaches, word tends to leak out to employees, and then it is almost impossible to contain it. Slow days at the office love bad news.

■ Plan to turn the breach into an awareness and training opportunity, as appropriate to the incident, and at the right time. That time will not likely be during the investigation phase. Take the time to take in the event, the response to the event, the cause or causes of the breach, the impact of it, its complexity, and other factors. Gaining perspective may take some time, and meaningful awareness and training will require the integration of that perspective. Mirroring life, education and learning are lifelong experiences. Learning from a breach event is no different.

2. Discovery and Forensic Evidence Capture

■ Begin the process to confirm that a breach has occurred and profile the scope and dimension of the breach point as soon as possible. It sounds easy to verify this assessment: that a breach has occurred. That is not the case, and some breaches go undetected for years. It is also not always possible to define the extent of the breach, so identifying the breach point is desirable, even preferable.

■ Determine the potential range of information that may be affected:
  ■ Personally identifying information (nonpublic personal information, or NPPI) such as protected health information
  ■ Credit card and financial account information
  ■ Employee family information, if applicable
  ■ Intellectual property, trade secrets, or other internal confidential business information
  ■ Jointly held business proprietary information:
    ■ Alliance partners, including government and industry
    ■ Customers
    ■ Third-party vendors
    ■ Investors

■ Examine the breach history of the company, if any, to evaluate any commonalities. It is possible that the current breach is similar to a prior breach, which may facilitate the identification of key indicators in the process of discovery.

■ If there is no internal breach history, look for similar breaches of regulated data at other companies in order to evaluate any commonalities. Search the Internet for similar cases: There are numerous cases posted on various industry and government web sites, often with substantial detail. Consider discussing this with any third-party vendors, too, because those firms may have experienced similar attack patterns.

■ Change passwords throughout the organization, using complex composition based on leading practices. While not a panacea, this should be an immediate response.

■ Determine if the breach is continuing or if it has stopped. This isn't always easy to know, but knowing the answer is essential.

■ Review insurance coverage. Cyber insurance is a rapidly evolving area, and it pays to keep up with the changes. Sometimes the insurance policies get reviewed only after a cyber event, which can lead to wrong conclusions based on a rush to judgment in interpretation. Examine the types of applicable insurance. It is also reasonable to bear in mind that a cyber breach may involve other types of accompanying threats, including the threat of physical violence, sexual assault, extortion and blackmail, and even kidnapping. Examine these insurance policies to verify coverage before the breach hits:

  ■ General liability
  ■ Technology errors and omissions
  ■ Directors' and officers' insurance
  ■ Cyber breach insurance

■ Determine if the breached data was encrypted. Oddly enough, sometimes the answer is unknown for a period of time. But it's important to know:

  ■ What encryption method was used
  ■ If the devices were encrypted at the file level or if full device encryption was used
  ■ Whether or not kill switches were installed on the devices, enabling them to be shut down and made inaccessible
  ■ Whether the data was accessible and readable at the time of compromise

■ Isolate and image any hard drives and begin forensic examination by a qualified external and independent professional. Be sure to require authorized access to the computer drives as a precaution in the event an insider with privileged access attempts to modify drive content. Ideally, all forensic analysis should be executed in a highly secure, zoned area, with enforced badging, monitoring, and appropriate surveillance.

3. Web Behavioral Analytics

■ Begin Web and behavioral analytics: Evaluate IP addresses, web sites, and e-mail addresses to assess the level of potential damage:

- Internal
- Third-party vendors
- Customers. This can be controversial since many companies under attack are often hesitant to share this information with customers. But sometimes toxic IP addresses from customers may be connected to the attack. Not notifying the customer may also increase the risk to the customer, who may not know of the toxic IP address presence.
- Categorize IP addresses by type:
  - **Type A.** Authorized by the company and its customers or other third parties and intended to be in the environment.
  - **Type B.** Unauthorized, toxic, with no valid reason for being in the environment.
  - **Type C.** Authorized by a third-party vendor or customer but toxic. The other party simply does not realize that the IP addresses are toxic. This is an indicator that they have been attacked and are likely unaware of that breach. The presence of toxic IP addresses from even a customer could mean that these are the IP addresses that could be broadcasting information out of the enterprise.
- Determine possible toxic IP address origination and ISP threat sources using various threat database tools:
  - Examine ISP selection and distribution. Certain ISPs are known to be unrestrictive and allow criminal or suspect traffic. If the ISP is found to be suspect in the attack, take immediate measures to cancel the agreement and seek alternative ISP providers.
  - Examine toxic IP address histories.
- Determine the source of the breach:
  - Internal:
    - Employee
    - Ex-employee
    - Third-party vendor employee or ex-employee
    - Independent contractor
    - Other
  - External:
    - Nation-state
    - Transnational organized crime
    - Hacker organization
    - Independent rogue hacker
    - Rogue individual
    - Other

- Determine if there are multiple breach points. This is an increasingly common condition and may lead to confusion and diagnostic error if not managed effectively and aggressively.
- Determine the method or methods of breach used to gain access to privileged data.
- Determine if the breach or attempted breach involved local proximity:
  - Was it a wireless signal intended to trick employees into clicking on the link and consequently downloading malware?
  - What was the source of proximity threat?
  - Was malware downloaded?
    - If yes:
      - By whom?
      - Has it spread throughout the enterprise, and could it still spread?
      - What was the nature and origin of the malware?
      - Are patches up to date?
      - What do the logs indicate?
  - Are known and unidentified wireless networks monitored and recorded for determination of origin and consistent presence?
- Physical intrusion:
  - Was a physical intrusion through perimeter security involved?
  - Does physical intrusion constitute a physical threat to employees or others?
  - Is video surveillance evidence available for analysis?
- Determine if a multidimensional, multivector threat is occurring.
- Are other physical plant locations experiencing suspect traffic or attack conditions? This could be an indicator of a diversified attack scenario or, alternatively, of an attempt to confuse the target and cause a diffuse allocation of defense assets.
- How integrated is the physical and logical threat detection system?
  - Internal and centralized versus decentralized
  - External and managed by a third party

4. Risk Impact Analysis

- Initiate a risk impact analysis and root cause analysis.
- Verify the type of data affected:
  - Intellectual property
  - Trade secrets

- Personally identifying information (PPI)
- Protected health information
- Examine paper and electronic record formats:
  - Look for user-defined fields that may contain personal information and that have not been cleansed of data.
  - Addressing paper records is important for several reasons. First, certain regulatory requirements pertain to paper records. Second, if there is an inside accomplice, a paper record may be less restricted and therefore more accessible and more at risk. Third, if an intruder is able to breach perimeter security but is unable to penetrate computers, paper records would be at risk.
- Determine if law enforcement notification is required or desired. Law enforcement triggers include:
  - Personally identifiable information (PII)
  - Personal health information (PHI)
  - Intellectual property and trade secrets
  - Information pertinent to critical infrastructure
  - Defense information. This may include the identities of any military personnel, which could be used in the commission of blackmail, ransom demands, or other crimes.
- Determine the requirement for specific government, law enforcement, and intelligence notification:
  - Federal Bureau of Investigation
  - Secret Service
  - Department of Defense Criminal Investigative Service
  - Immigration and Customs Enforcement
  - Drug Enforcement Administration
  - Department of Homeland Security
  - Department of State
  - National Cyber-Forensics and Training Alliance
  - IC3 (Internet Crime Complaint Center)
  - Central Intelligence Agency
  - State police
  - Local police
- Define internal reporting requirements with external consulting and/or legal adviser:
  - Daily or weekly progress read-outs:
    - Attendees list:

- ▪ Required
- ▪ Desired
- ▪ Preparation of interim reports for discussion with:
  - ▪ Law enforcement
  - ▪ Regulators
  - ▪ At-risk corporate customers or clients and partners
  - ▪ Board members
- ▪ Develop a tactical plan for point-of-breach containment, which is always a consideration in:
  - ▪ Regulator negotiation
  - ▪ Insurer presentment
  - ▪ Corporate customer contract negotiation
- ▪ Examine corporate agreements, including service level agreements and business associate agreements, to determine contract obligations and reporting requirements, which may be separate from regulatory reporting requirements:
  - ▪ Determine contract client or customer and regulator notification strategy. Determine notification based on specified requirements. For example, some agreements require notification based on determination of a breach based on regulatory requirements. Other notifications are based on a negotiated agreement between parties. This is why it is critical to actually define the term "breach" and then specify the notification timing and format.
  - ▪ Create a regulator and client negotiation framework based on breach circumstances, findings on vulnerabilities, threat vectors, and remediation strategy.
- ▪ Examine the enterprise risk management framework to determine consistency and effectiveness.
- ▪ Examine policies and procedures for information security and privacy and compliance.
- ▪ Establish regulatory reporting procedures in case such notification becomes a requirement:
  - ▪ Regulators:
    - ▪ State
    - ▪ Federal
    - ▪ Industry
    - ▪ Foreign country
  - ▪ Corporate customers
  - ▪ Consumers

- Determine appropriate negotiation strategies based on breach circumstances, institutional deficiencies, and remediation strategies.
- Determine requirements for temporary restraining orders/abuse reports and execute accordingly:
  - Examine target ISP deployment.
  - Examine web sites and search engines participating in breached data distribution.
  - Determine country-level government cooperation.
  - Determine if alliance partners in the United States may be valuable in the application of pressure against foreign ISPs, web sites, and search engines as part of breach analysis.

5. Reporting to Constituent Groups

- First, work with legal counsel and other independent advisers to determine the appropriate audience for any reporting. One common mistake made by companies is that the investigative process is a strictly technical analysis. It is true that the attack and the analysis of it is technical in orientation, but that is only one aspect of what needs to be conveyed. Sending technical information to an untechnical audience may result in frustration and inaccurate conclusions. An executive summary for the nontechnical audience, including members of the board of directors, is essential. When writing executive reports, it is vital to use the language of the business and of risk. Avoid losing the audience with overly technical language. While it is true that more senior executives and board members are more attuned to cyber-related issues, senior management and the board will often be more responsive to the management of risk than the management of technology. Many organizations make the fundamental mistake of creating only technical documentation. In large part this is due to the technical nature of the breach and the deployment of technical staff to investigate the breach. But an executive summary for a nontechnical audience is vital.
- It is important to remember that there will likely be a diverse set of readers for the report. Among the readers may be insurers, law enforcement, company executives, key shareholders, various regulators, nontechnical corporate customers, external legal counsel representing various interests, internal auditors of multiple companies, strategic partners, third-party vendors, and others. Accessibility to the importance of the report is

essential, so the report should be sufficiently accessible to a varied business audience.

- The executive report should contain the following sections:
  - **Introduction** highlighting general risk conditions and trends.
  - **Description of the breached company**, markets served, products and services offered, global reach, and so on. Again, the audience may be diverse and not necessarily understand the business of the company.
  - **Description of the intrusion event** based on forensic examination and Web and behavioral analytics.
  - **Date of intrusion**. There may be multiple dates over a protracted time period. In some cases, given either the sophistication of an attack or the deficiencies of the targeted organization's intrusion detection and prevention capabilities, the dates of intrusion may be difficult or impossible to calculate. In many documented cases, the breach activity remained undetected for years. But every effort should be made to accurately identify intrusion dates.
  - **Description of at-risk data**, regulated and unregulated. Be as detailed as possible. Not all paper and electronic records are in the same format. Be prepared to provide specific examples of information and record types.
  - **Analysis of preliminary mitigation measures**. This is key for the structuring of successful negotiations with corporate customers and regulators and a reduction of risk impact.
  - Breach containment analysis:
    - Completed
    - In process
    - Scheduled
    - Unscheduled
- **Conclusions and recommendations**. Documenting conclusions and subsequent recommendations is important to various constituent groups, including executive management and the board of directors. It is also crucial in discussions with regulators and corporate customers. Conclusions must be detailed as well as thoughtful, reflecting a meaningful level of effort. This will help in convincing regulators and customers of the institution's commitment to effectively manage risk impact. In cases where there is an insufficient demonstration of careful planning and execution of the breach investigation, there may be increased regulatory inquiry and pushback from corporate customers whose data may be impacted. The failure to convince corporate customers and

regulators of the level of effort applied may result in increased breach-related costs, impaired reputation, and the loss of business and even corporate valuation.

■ **Technical summary** (actual reporting structure may vary by type of attack). Absolutely fundamental in understanding the event, the technical report will have value to the technical audience:

  ■ Introduction
  ■ Review of suspicious IP addresses, e-mails, Web activity, and so on
  ■ Summary
  ■ Details as appropriate to the breach event:
    ■ Threat source
    ■ Vulnerabilities
    ■ Breach enablement
  ■ Recommendations
  ■ Forensic review and analysis of selected computer hard drives:
    ■ Summary
    ■ Detail
  ■ Recommendations
  ■ Scanning and vulnerability tests:
    ■ Summary
    ■ Detailed technical findings
    ■ Conclusions and recommendations

One of the worst mistakes that can be made is the failure to act quickly and decisively. Failure to act quickly and decisively is usually due to one of two conditions: Either the preparations for launching an investigation are inadequate, and precious time is lost trying to gear up for the effort, or it isn't clear that a breach is taking place because signals of the breach are missed entirely. Some companies don't monitor logs very well, and signals coming from the logs can easily be missed—especially if no one is watching and analyzing the contents of the logs.

No one wants a breach. Almost all organizations are likely to experience one. Many of those experiencing a breach will make mistakes in risk assessment, breach severity, what to report, when to report it, how to report it, and to whom it should be reported. There is no substitute for being prepared, and being prepared will pay dividends when it comes time for disclosure. And that's the thing about a breach. All breaches will probably be reported to someone.

CHAPTER NINE

Managing the Big Risk

Third-Party Vendors

The golden rule for every business man [or
woman] is this: "Put yourself in your customer's
place."

—*Orison Swett Marden, American author*

D ESPITE MARDEN'S advice, it does not seem to be often that this
occurs. This chapter, on the risks associated with engaging third-
party vendors, is titled "Managing the Big Risk." The reason it is
called the Big Risk is that it *is* a big risk, perhaps the biggest. Third parties
introduce a variety of risks into virtually every environment. Small and
large companies alike use multiple third-party vendors. Some companies
use literally thousands of third-party vendors to assist in a wide range of
operations. While some third parties simply engage with companies to come
in on a periodic basis to tend to the office plants or to exchange empty
drinking water containers for full ones, others perform a wide array of
information-related services that involve highly sensitive information.

Some third-party vendors are the proverbial back door, a door with
perhaps less security, less reinforcement, fewer locks, a lower level of

awareness, and less due diligence applied. This adds up to more risk. In an environment where security is strong, attackers would likely move to an alternative strategy. Sometimes this means that they attack through a third-party vendor.

Expect that the relationship between companies and third-party vendors is going to be on the fast track to change. Already the federal government is pressing for vendor management changes. Financial institutions and health care organizations are grappling with changes to the spirit and letter of increasingly restrictive regulations. Strengthening privacy regulations in the European Union will unquestionably exert influence over U.S. state and federal regulations that are, generally, less robust.

Federal and state government regulators of both financial services and health care industries are cognizant of the increasing risk posed by third-party vendors and are taking action. One of the regulations that addresses third-party vendor risk and responsibility is the health care Omnibus Final Rule, part of the Health Insurance Portability and Accountability Act (HIPAA). It was passed into law in March 2013 and the date for compliance was September of that year. But as with many regulations, the rate of compliance will not be as high as the Department of Health and Human Services would like it to be. This rule has a significant impact on third parties, or, as specified in the rule, "business associates." The 563-page rule sets the stage for future information management practices.

The Office for Civil Rights of the Department of Health and Human Services describes the Omnibus Final Rule as "the most sweeping changes to the HIPAA Privacy and Security Rules since they were first implemented." Business associates are now required to take responsibility for their subcontractors, an area of historical concern when it comes to third parties. Business associates must abide by the security and breach notification rules.[1]

The Federal Deposit Insurance Corporation (FDIC) links third-party vendors to reputation risk. FDIC guidance states that "reputation risk is the risk arising from negative public opinion. Third-party relationships that result in . . . security breaches resulting in the disclosure of customer information are . . . examples that could harm the reputation and standing of the institution. Any negative publicity involving the third party, whether or not the publicity is related to the institution's use of the third party, could result in reputation risk."

The guidance also links third-party vendors to operational risk, "the risk of loss resulting from inadequate or failed internal processes, people, systems, or external events. Third-party relationships often integrate the internal processes of other organizations with the institution's processes and can increase the overall operational complexity."[2]

The FDIC has issued recommendations on conducting vendor due diligence, practices that all companies should commit to in examining the suitability of third-party vendors. The evaluation of a third party may include the following:

- Audited financial statements, annual reports, Securities and Exchange Commission filings, and other available financial information;
- Significance of the proposed contract on the third party's financial condition;
- Experience and ability in implementing and monitoring the proposed activity;
- Business reputation, including any complaints filed;
- Span of business operations in which the third party is engaged;
- Qualifications and experience of the company's principals;
- Strategies and goals, including service philosophies, quality initiatives, efficiency improvements, and employment policies;
- Existence of any significant complaints or litigation (past and pending) or supervisory actions against the company or its owners or principals;
- Ability to perform the proposed functions using current systems or the need to make additional investments;
- Use of other parties or subcontractors by the third party;
- Scope of internal controls, systems and data security, privacy protections, and audit coverage;
- Business resumption strategy and contingency plans;
- Knowledge of, and background and experience with, consumer protection and civil rights laws and regulations;
- Underwriting criteria;
- Adequacy of management information systems;
- Insurance coverage;
- Marketing materials to determine how the institution's name will be associated with the product;
- Web sites; and
- Vendor and institution management responsibilities.

Third-party companies contract with companies to manage e-mail lists, patient data, and financial information, and also often have direct access to extremely sensitive intellectual property and trade secrets. It is hard to imagine conducting business in the twenty-first century without the assistance of third-party vendors. Their use allows companies to more successfully manage head count and budgets, and to contract and expand more readily in response to market reduction and growth. In the case of outsourcing, there are tremendous financial incentives to use lower-cost resources. The use of offshore third parties has become so widespread that a few years ago one venture capital firm partner on the West Coast was quoted as saying that his firm didn't bother to read any business plans that didn't outsource certain work to low-cost providers overseas.

There's no question that outsourcing to other countries introduces new security and risk management issues into the corporate agenda. But outsourcing to domestic vendors is also not without risk. The story of the NSA leaks of 2013 shed light on this subject. Remember, Edward Snowden worked for a third-party vendor! While it remains uncertain what exactly Mr. Snowden shared with other nations, we do know that he wasn't authorized to disclose classified information. Some may believe he is a hero, others that he is a villain. It is clear, though, that his employer is the recipient of unwanted publicity. The company is one of the more prominent government contractors supplying personnel to the intelligence community.

It is also clear that the third-party background investigation firm that vetted Mr. Snowden is under examination. Northern Virginia–based USIS, which advertises that it is "the leader in federal background investigations," is on the hot seat. Senator Claire McCaskill said during a Senate hearing in June 2013 that USIS is "under active criminal investigation."

Additional details in this case will come forward as the investigation continues. But much of the information around this case will undoubtedly be classified, with only limited disclosure in the media and in public congressional hearings. But what is exceedingly clear is that egregious mistakes were made. The contractual obligations between third parties and the NSA failed.

Senator McCaskill also noted that there appeared to be a "systemic failure to adequately conduct investigations under its contract." In a statement that should resonate with every company engaging with third-party background investigation services, Senator McCaskill commented that this should serve as "a reminder that background investigations can have real consequences for our national security." The problem extends to companies outside of the Washington Beltway and the defense and intelligence arena.

While it may be unlikely that third-party employee behavior will rise to the level of policy violation exhibited by Mr. Snowden, it doesn't have to in order to compromise information integrity, breach corporate governance and contracts, and violate regulatory requirements in the forms of identity theft, trade secret theft, brand hijacking, blackmail, and extortion. The background investigation doesn't always work.

The annals of background investigation history are rich with examples of failed policies, procedures, and even strategies associated with understanding the truth about a candidate's past. Criminals have passed background checks. There is a reason that Top Secret security clearances can take up to nearly two years to conduct and may cost several thousand dollars, and sometimes much more, depending on a number of variables related to each case. Of course, not every candidate needs this level of background investigation. But companies should examine the background investigation process used by third parties that have physical, logical, or administrative access to information.

It's always good to conduct a more extensive background investigation on the basis of access. Sometimes organizations initiate background checks only on some candidates. One executive remarked that "we only conduct checks on positions with the title of vice president or above." This can convey a false sense of security. While senior executives may have access to critical sensitive information, many lower-level positions come with high levels of access to the same information.

One of these variables is the background investigation process, which is many times a flawed process based on a flawed strategy.

BACKGROUND INVESTIGATION SUGGESTIONS TO IMPROVE PROCESS

The FDIC recommends 10 background investigation considerations:

1. Assess how the third party under consideration may pose a risk to your company, not by the title or level of a position, but rather by the level of access to information.
2. Make sure the third party is open and responsive to questioning about the background check process. Trust but verify, as the saying goes.
3. Ask about their background investigation vendors, and then conduct your own due diligence on those firms used by the third parties. Examine the processes and methods used to investigate candidates.
4. Don't hesitate to ask to see background-check forms. We've seen background reports where certain information contained in the report didn't seem right—and it wasn't. Maybe it was a phone number that didn't seem

correct, perhaps an area code that doesn't exist. Yes, people actually make up telephone numbers and addresses. It may be worth knowing what type of telephone number was used by the candidate. Is it a temporary, prepaid number? Is it a registered mobile number, a home telephone, or maybe even a business telephone number? Is it the number of a family member, a friend, or other person?

5. Have the third-party firm supply references. And make sure that the references are consistent with your company. For example, if the third party is going to handle regulated data, check out companies that have engaged the third party to manage that type of information. The security and privacy requirements may be industry- or jurisdiction-specific.

6. Check the third-party breach history and the cause of any breaches. Were any breaches linked to failures in the background investigation process?

7. Ask what lessons were learned after any breaches and if those lessons were incorporated into the background analysis process.

8. Are employees ever reinvestigated?

9. What is the reinvestigation frequency and scope?

10. Are reinvestigations triggered by certain life events, or corporate events, such as a merger or acquisition?

The accuracy and effectiveness of background investigations of third-party employees is one of the best defenses against a breach and its consequences. Knowing who has access to your data, and whether they are trustworthy, is a mandatory tenet of strong corporate governance.

Failed background investigations have led to breaches of regulated information, from protected health information to customer financial information. In some cases there were complete breakdowns in the background investigation process, in which convicted felons passed criminal background checks. Almost unbelievably, such failures included company contractors who did not actually exist yet were still able to pass background checks. An enterprising entrepreneur created these identities, giving them names, addresses, cell phone numbers, and even Social Security numbers, and saw to it that each passed a basic background check. Enterprising, yes, but quite illegal, and these "contractors" and their creator were stealing customer financial information.

Who's to blame? As in many breaches of regulated data, as well as intellectual property and trade secrets, there is plenty of blame to go around. Companies often hold third-party vendors accountable only after there has been a breach. These same companies often conduct due diligence on third parties, but too frequently the process of determining the risk associated with any one third party is too costly and time-consuming. Plus, many vendors will simply walk away from companies that press too hard on the issue of security. Many of these third parties, and the companies that contract with them, will meet at the bar of accountability and information protection established by law and implemented by regulation. If a company utilizes hundreds or even thousands of vendors, it becomes difficult to manage them individually, at least until there has been a breach.

Another issue seen frequently is that many executives have long-standing relationships with preferred third parties. "We've been using them for 20 years and there haven't been any problems yet. We'll keep using them." This is quite common, even when detailed due diligence clearly illustrates that the continued use of the third-party vendor elevates company risk. Sometimes the executive of the company and the vendor worked together previously and feel that loyalty is at stake, even if the corporate risk rises.

What the company executives either don't know or ignore in the hope that nothing bad will happen is that things change. This is especially true in the case of a long-term relationship. Nothing stays the same. Management changes, employees come and go, maybe some work goes overseas, some outsourced to other companies domestically. Regulations, standards, guidelines change, as do the efforts made by vendors to comply with the requirements of change. The financial integrity of the vendor could have changed: It could be near bankruptcy, or it could be the target of civil litigation or even criminal prosecution. When change happens, it's always a good bet to make sure that the change reduces risk, not elevates it.

Here's another thing. Statistics vary about the total percentage of third parties involved in data breaches. Some authorities suggest the number of breaches involving third parties is more than half, some less than half. Actually, the specific number isn't terribly important, but the trend is very important. The trend seems to point to an increase, perhaps because third-party vendors are managing more and more data. But here's another statistic, although not a broadly based one: In every breach investigation conducted by this author a third party has been involved in the breach. Every one. While this is admittedly anecdotal, when examining the entire industry it does illustrate the severity of the problem.

Third-party vendor relationships are typically managed through service level agreements. The problem? Many such agreements are drafted with a specific emphasis on legal enforcement provisions should the vendor fail to meet certain contractual requirements, productivity goals, and mandated regulatory minimum requirements for information protection and breach notification. This applies only to personal information that is subject to various government regulations. For vendors in possession of intellectual property and trade secrets, the last category, information protection and breach notification, may be absent or nonspecific because of no—or limited—obligatory public reporting requirements.

Before contracting with third parties, companies should carefully evaluate the risks of engaging third parties to manage certain kinds of information, who will have access to that information, where the information will reside, how it will be transported, whether it will cross jurisdictional lines, what regulations apply, what is the vendor's breach track record, and more. Many companies conduct extensive due diligence, pressing during the due diligence phase, asking hundreds of questions and demanding satisfactory answers and demonstrations of proof.

It may be helpful to shift from service level agreements to something like a risk-reinforced service level agreement (RRSLA). While many firms do a reasonable job in the due diligence phase, it seems, many do not, and this seems especially true in many smaller and midsize companies. RRLSAs focus on seven specific, detailed assessment points that assist the company in casting a broad net, yet a comprehensive one, over the third-party vendor relationship. In each of the seven points, which are discussed below, a detailed set of requirements is established, and so is documentation and the establishment of frequency of testing.

Companies must require documentation from vendors, demonstrations of proof that vendors have done what they said they were going to do and when they said they were going to do it. It isn't uncommon for companies to sign SLAs with vendors that state that the vendors must agree to specific requirements. Yet the reality is that companies many times do not check up on their third-party vendors, even when the SLA requires compliance with state and federal regulations governing information protection and breach notification requirements.

The result can be that the SLA, after being signed at the beginning of the relationship, is sometimes never looked at again by either party until the time comes to renew the agreement. There can be significant consequences to this. There are cases where (1) the SLA was signed by an employee, not an officer, of the third-party vendor; (2) the vendor was obligated to be compliant with U.S. federal, state, and international data privacy regulations but did not understand that it needed to be compliant; (3) the company never initially requested documentation demonstrating compliance and never did until a breach occurred. The breach in this case was significant. While the data management provider was at fault, there is no question that the company's customers shared in the blame. The customers failed to hold the vendor accountable by conducting effective due diligence, not only prior to signing the agreement but on a regular basis thereafter. Had the customers checked, the security lapses and failure to comply with both government regulatory requirements and contractual obligations would have been evident. It is likely that such due diligence would have reduced the impact of the breach, and perhaps would have prevented it altogether.

Of course, as with any program, there are varying levels of details defining each agreement. Every company must make a decision on how much detail to require. Admittedly, managing an increased flow of documentation isn't necessarily easy, and it can be costly as well. But the point is that today many companies are failing to make informed decisions about what they need to know about their service providers. Every company needs to make informed decisions about what to require, when to require, and how much documentation they need to review. It comes down to the company's appetite for third-party vendor risk.

This can be a difficult balance to achieve, based on innumerable criteria. Not all vendors need to have the same level of scrutiny. The measure of due diligence to be expended depends on what information will be in the possession of the third-party vendor and what services are offered by the vendor.

For personal financial data, the principal federal protective instrument is the Gramm-Leach-Bliley Act of 1999, also known as the Financial Services Modernization Act of 1999. A key component of the act is what is known as the Safeguards Rule. This is important for client companies as well as third-party vendors, because ultimately it is the client company's responsibility to protect the privacy of information. The Safeguards Rule requires companies to develop a written information security plan that describes their program to protect customer information. The plan must be appropriate to the company's size and complexity, the nature and scope of its activities, and the sensitivity of the customer information it handles. As part of its plan, each company must:

- Designate one or more employees to coordinate its information security program;
- Identify and assess the risks to customer information in each relevant area of the company's operation, and evaluate the effectiveness of the current safeguards for controlling those risks;

- Design and implement a safeguards program, and regularly monitor and test it; and
- Select service providers that can maintain appropriate safeguards, make sure the contract requires them to maintain safeguards, and oversee their handling of customer information; and evaluate and adjust the program in light of relevant circumstances, including changes in the firm's business or operations or the results of security testing and monitoring.

 ## RISK-REINFORCED SERVICE LEVEL AGREEMENTS

While the following is not intended to be a comprehensive instrument for managing third-party vendor risk, it does identify seven key risk issues to consider including in any SLA, turning it into a risk-reinforced service level agreement. These requirements are intentionally vague, allowing each company, based on its size and requirements, to develop its program within the required framework. Every company should develop its own RRSLA based on many individual factors making up its risk profile. Regulatory requirements, type of data at risk, budget, risk tolerance, and other factors will be considered in determining the level of effort that will be placed in the development of the RRSLA. The key is to make sure the third-party vendor is on board with the program. Here are the seven basic elements for consideration:

1. **Information security.** Information security is not the same as IT security, though the two terms are often used interchangeably. The difference between the two is one of both regulatory language and practical perspective. Under most regulatory guidelines, information security is comprised of technical or logical security, physical security, and administrative security. In a risk-reinforced service level agreement, it is important to make sure that all three types of security are recognized by the vendor. Information security requirements should be formalized and written in easy-to-understand language. Linking requirements to standards, regulations, and guidelines is important. The noteworthy standards and guidelines include the credit card requirement known as PCI DSS, or the Payment Card Industry Data Security Standard. PCI DSS applies to any organization that accepts, acquires, transmits, processes, or stores data that contains payment card information. The National Institute of Standards Technology (NIST), originally developed to help U.S. federal government agencies meet the requirements of the

Federal Information Security Management Act (FISMA), is an excellent guideline. Many private-sector organizations use many elements of NIST to manage security operations. Another respected security standard is the International Standards Organization (ISO) 27000 security standard. These are not the only standards and guidelines, but they are valuable resources. Many companies use elements of multiple information security resources in order to more meaningfully manage risk. Some of the best frameworks governing third-party vendors are borrowed from multiple resources.

Information security is the foundation for managing operational risk, so make this a priority when dealing with vendors and service level agreements. In other words:

a. Be specific.

b. Be detailed.

c. Require regular reporting at reasonable, agreed-upon intervals. Even if the vendor fails to report, at least you have requested such meetings and reporting, which will prove useful in the event you need to deflect risk back to the vendor in the event of a cyber breach.

d. Require written reporting in the form of documentation that meets regulatory as well as insurer requirements.

e. Negotiate until satisfaction has been achieved. It is your risk and the company's risk.

f. If it is impossible to negotiate successfully there may come a point at which it is time to disengage. Perhaps the vendor will give, perhaps not. But the issue is that it is unwise to accept risk beyond the risk tolerance established by the board of directors and the senior management team.

g. Hold the vendors to the letter of the service level agreement. The key is in making certain that the SLA is tight and reflects the actual risk management goals.

2. **Information privacy.** A variety of U.S. federal, state, and foreign-country legislation governs the protection and privacy requirements of personal information. There are good resources available for the framework for managing information privacy, which should be reviewed when crafting any third-party vendor service level agreement. The Generally Accepted Privacy Principles (GAPP) represent a good starting point in examining privacy management. GAPP was developed by the American Institute of Certified Public Accounts (AICPA) and the Canadian Institute of Chartered Accountants (CICA). GAPP has a reasonable business

definition of privacy. It states, "Privacy is defined in Generally Accepted Privacy Principles as 'the rights and obligations of individuals and organizations with respect to the collection, use, retention, disclosure and disposal of personal information.'" GAPP establishes general categories of privacy as a frame of reference, which should be factored in:

- Information on medical or health conditions
- Financial information
- Racial or ethnic origin
- Political opinions
- Religious or philosophical beliefs
- Trade union membership
- Sexual preference
- Information related to offenses or criminal convictions

GAPP articulates 10 useful privacy principles, which are essential to any organization and are especially important in developing the third-party vendor service level agreement:

a. **Management.** The entity defines, documents, communicates, and assigns accountability for its privacy policies and procedures.

b. **Notice.** The entity provides notice about its privacy policies and procedures and identifies the purposes for which personal information is collected, used, retained, and disclosed.

c. **Choice and consent.** The entity describes the choices available to the individual and obtains implicit or explicit consent with respect to the collection, use, and disclosure of personal information.

d. **Collection.** The entity collects personal information only for the purposes identified in the notice.

e. **Use, retention, and disposal.** The entity limits the use of personal information to the purposes identified in the notice and for which the individual has provided implicit or explicit consent. The entity retains personal information for only as long as necessary to fulfill the stated purposes or as required by law or regulation and thereafter appropriately disposes of such information.

f. **Access.** The entity provides individuals with access to their personal information for review and update.

g. **Disclosure to third parties.** The entity discloses personal information to third parties only for the purposes identified in the notice and with the implicit or explicit consent of the individual.

h. **Security for privacy.** The entity protects personal information against unauthorized access (both physical and logical).

i. **Quality.** The entity maintains accurate, complete, and relevant personal information for the purposes identified in the notice.

j. **Monitoring and enforcement.** The entity monitors compliance with its privacy policies and procedures and has procedures to address privacy-related complaints and disputes.

Define information privacy for the vendor, and how it must be observed and managed. Information privacy is about how regulated information may be used and by whom. There are a great many variables, especially by country. Information privacy in the European Union, for example, is substantially more restrictive than in the United States. Define personally identifiable information (PII) for all applicable vendors. PII is diversified and includes, generally, the following types of information:

a. Health care data (PHI, or protected health information)
   1. Names.
   2. All geographical subdivisions smaller than a state, including street address, city, county, precinct, zip code, if the "geographic unit formed by combining all zip codes within the same three initial digits contains more than 20,000 people; and the initial three digits of a zip code for all such geographic units containing 20,000 or fewer people is changed to 000."
   3. All elements of dates, except year, for dates directly related to an individual, including birth date, admission date, discharge date, date of death; and all ages over 89 and all elements of dates (including year) indicative of such age, except that such ages and elements may be aggregated into a single category of age 90 or older.
   4. Phone numbers.
   5. Fax numbers.
   6. E-mail addresses.
   7. Social Security numbers.
   8. Medical record numbers.
   9. Health plan beneficiary numbers.
   10. Account numbers.
   11. Certificate/license numbers.
   12. Vehicle identifiers and serial numbers, including license plate numbers.
   13. Device identifiers and serial numbers.
   14. Web uniform resource locators (URLs).
   15. Internet protocol (IP) addresses.
   16. Biometric identifiers, including fingerprints and voice prints.

17. Full-face photographic images and any comparable images; and
18. Any other unique identifying number, characteristic, or code.
19. It should also be noted that there are additional standards and criteria to protect an individual's privacy from what is called reidentification, according to the Committee on Human Research at the University of California. What this means is that any code that is used to replace the identifiers in datasets cannot be derived from any information related to the individual and the master codes, nor can the method to derive the codes be disclosed.

b. Genetic data
c. Ethnicity
d. Criminal proceedings
e. Geolocation data
f. Other

But GAPP is also about unregulated data, including intellectual property and trade secrets, which need to be kept confidential. Information privacy means not only protecting the information from theft, but also protecting it from compromise such as change in the data. So information integrity must be part of the mission to ensure that information is guarded, from inside and outside the vendor environment. Specify what data needs to be protected! Make reference to what data is regulated by law and what must be done to protect that information. Most important, make certain that there is an understanding with the third-party vendor on what the requirement is to treat information in their custody. Included should be information in any digital form, as well as information in paper form. This is no time to be vague or imprecise. Don't let the vendor make any assumptions: Stick to the facts as you define them.

3. **Threat and risk analysis.** A number of regulations require that companies, and therefore third-party vendors, perform risk assessment. Don't just casually accept any risk assessment conducted by a third-party vendor. Remember that the goal is not just to meet—and have third-party vendors meet—a regulatory requirement. The goal is to protect information and see that others entrusted with that responsibility protect it, too.

Make it meaningful. Make sure that the analysis of risk is linked to the actual threats facing the company and the third-party vendor. For example, consider the insider threat. What has the vendor done to measure that risk? How carefully have such vendors examined their own background investigation process? What are the actual threats that have been considered in their risk assessment? Have they looked at the full spectrum of likely threats facing them? How have these threats been interpreted in terms of risk? Have they examined the legal, regulatory, financial, and reputation risk arising from an event?

Determine from where the vendors are receiving threat information. Is it consistent with what is required to actually protect information? Here's an example. Suppose that the vendor has offshore operations and that data is under management there. Then suppose that the country is one with a significant level of corruption, organized crime, narcotics trafficking, social protest, and so on. In instances where there is heightened corruption, fraud, and other criminal activity, there is greater risk. Then consider how technology and culture enhance the threat and the risk to companies. How does the third-party vendor manage its employees and contractors with respect to the use of social media? Does the vendor have a "bring your own device" policy? There's the risk of hiring employees and contractors who may be engaged in illegal and unethical activities, or who are simply careless with the information they post on social media sites and keep on their personal devices. Consider if the principal company factored these concerns into its own risk equation, and then factor this into the third-party vendor risk.

A word about the social protest threat. Social protest, in most cases, is legal, and even desirable. It is a fundamental precept of a free country. However, many protest groups have the desire and the ability to disrupt the flow of information. It is also well established that hacker groups, and even terrorist groups, try to co-opt some protest groups. So the real issue is not that a region or a country may have active social protest groups, but whether those protests have the ability to interfere or disrupt information management. If so, what mitigation measures have been put in place by the third-party vendor? Have those measures been evaluated and tested? Has the need for change in policies or monitoring been required?

Another measure of the threat and risk conditions at the third-party vendor is the breach history. While many vendors are reluctant or intractable on the issue of such disclosures, it should be a point for negotiation between parties. But let's define breach. A breach is not only a breach of data that must be reported to state, federal, and foreign-country authorities. Many breaches, for a variety of reasons, are never reported to regulators. For the purposes of negotiation and agreement in a written contract, a breach should also be defined as a breach of security policy and procedure.

This requires the third-party vendor to disclose not only its breach history regarding regulated data, but also, if specified, any security incidents or breaches involving intellectual property and trade secrets. Making a decision about a third-party vendor, if it is to be handling any type of sensitive information, requires understanding its threat environment and the risk potential. Arriving at a decision about its suitability to handle that information simply cannot be done without understanding the full dimension of its historical risk performance. If the vendor decides that it should refrain from answering these probing questions, then the client company can at least make an informed decision about whether or not to engage a specific vendor.

There's often a gap between what companies and their third-party vendors believe is important. Understanding the threat and risk environment shouldn't be one of those gap areas. One of the best ways to think through the process of creating a trusted vendor relationship is simply this: Think postbreach, act prebreach. In other words, think about managing the risk from the perspective of a severe data breach. How could the breach have been averted? What steps could have been taken, what policy changes would have prevented the breach? Was it a technology issue? An organizational management issue? Was there a violation of regulation?

4. **Regulatory and industry compliance.** One of the measures of a third-party vendor's ability to successfully manage information risk is its regulatory and industry standard obligation to do so. Admittedly, the ability to comply with regulatory requirements around security and privacy is an example of mandatory minimum compliance. That may seem like a reasonably low bar. And maybe it is. But there are a few things to consider. First, many regulations are being strengthened, and at just about every level: federal, state, foreign country. This doesn't necessary mean that these regulations will be successful in preventing data breaches, but it does mean that companies will be held to a higher standard and that the mandatory minimum will be enhanced. However, regulation will never rise to the highest level of information protection, and that should also be considered. Second, a mandatory minimum is better than no minimum. Third, it provides a metric of measurement. Fourth, in cases of reported breaches, it is easier to determine how the breach occurred and what was done to mitigate that risk going forward.

5. **Internal audit.** Negotiate for as much access to the third-party vendor's internal audit reports as possible. These reports can be invaluable in

determining how the company audits itself, what it is able to detect and prevent, and what it has not been successful in detecting and preventing. Additionally, require the third party to accept a provision in the service level agreement for audit on demand by the client company. This requirement is especially important in certain foreign countries, where the internal audit process by the third-party vendor may not be as accurate as it may be in other countries. Being able to audit on demand that third party is important because it minimizes the opportunity for the vendor to obfuscate, and maximizes the ability of the client to probe virtually any aspect of the operation. Depending on the size and expanse of the client company, the audits may be conducted by professionals in-country or within the region. Or, alternatively, dispatching a team from corporate headquarters may be an option. It's important to make sure that the third-party vendor understands the language of the client company.

6. **Foreign corrupt practices management.** As mentioned elsewhere in this book, understanding the potential for corruption is increasingly important. This is, absolutely, an area well understood by the board of directors. A number of nations are cracking down on corruption, but it still exists. Refer to the Transparency International Corruption Perceptions Index when determining the prevalence of corruption in a particular country. While it is not an exact measure, and is based on perception, it is a useful metric in measuring and managing risk.

Examine the third-party vendor's whistleblower program. Not every company has such a program, but they have proven to be effective tools in managing the risks associated with corruption. Whistleblower programs provide an outlet for employees to alert management of bribery and other corrupt practices. Have the vendor disclose the program details. Minimally, require the vendor to disclose:

- When did the program go into effect?
- Who, by title, is ultimately responsible for managing it and overseeing it?
- Is it anonymous?
- How is the whistleblower protected?
- Is the program deployed in multiple jurisdictions?
- Is each jurisdiction monitored for regulatory changes?
- How is information conveyed in the program: e-mail, web site, telephone, text message, and so on?
- What is the use history and frequency?
- What actions were taken?
- What was the resolution?

Increasingly, corruption is a critical element in successfully managing reputation risk. As in the case of data breaches, findings of corruption can have a variety of risk impacts on any company. The business press, in particular, has demonstrated an interest in covering corruption, and is usually aggressive in its coverage.

It is important to work with legal counsel on this issue. Make sure that the anticorruption program covers every country in which the third party operates. Oftentimes the client company does not verify the details of the third-party anticorruption program or verify any history of corruption in the third party. While larger client enterprises are more likely to have an anticorruption requirement and program to verify the details specific to the third-party vendor, many small and midsize companies lack this critical due diligence effort. Minimally, it is important to at least have the vendor verify in writing:

- The existence of the vendor's anticorruption program, its mission statement, and its operational framework.
- Its history of anticorruption measures and any legal or regulatory actions taken against the vendor regarding corruption.
- Whether there is any pending litigation or regulatory action specific to corruption in any country.
- If there is pending litigation or regulatory action, whether that will have the potential to in any way imperil the reputation of the client company.
- The scope beyond vendor verification. Conduct an online search of the media to independently verify, to the extent possible, any information about the company and its relation to any corruption. While it may be less likely that large, reputable vendors may purposefully not disclose any such information, there are some vendors that may be less likely to make such a disclosure. It is also not unheard of for large third-party vendors whose operations span dozens of nations not to possess current knowledge about actions taken in foreign jurisdictions. This is why it is important to actually look at how such programs are monitored on an ongoing basis.
- Whether the program is an element of the vendor's corporate governance program, and how often it is addressed.

7. **Enforcement.** In the event the third-party vendor fails to meet the requirements laid out in the service level agreement, it is necessary to have an enforcement program in place. Enforcement should be proportionate to the event. It should be reasonable. Few companies are going to cancel

an agreement because its third-party vendor lost a BlackBerry with a few customer names on it. Of course, the circumstances and the profile of the lost identities always play a role in the outcome. However, a major breach of personal information or the loss of highly valuable intellectual property or trade secrets is a different story.

In one case, an executive signed a lucrative third-party vendor agreement with an old friend. They had worked together previously in another company. An after-the-fact assessment of the third-party vendor's security illustrated a number of crucial deficiencies. The scope and dimension of these deficiencies would clearly lead to a data breach at some point, and maintaining the agreement was not justifiable. It cost the company a substantial amount of money to get out of this contract because there were no real enforcement measures in place.

The client company should have made provisions in the contract about vendor security as a condition for agreement cancellation. But it wasn't there. Not only was there a difficult business negotiation, but it likely stressed a friendship as well.

In part, this is a decision that should be discussed in the risk committee of the board of directors as part of an information governance program. Information is valuable. In some companies it is the dominant value. In some companies it is also the prevailing risk. The risk committee of the board, especially if it is well informed, would want to know about which companies are handling its data. Too much detail for the risk committee? In the event of a breach, one that proved costly in regulatory, legal, financial, and reputation risk, who would want to be the bearer of the bad news? The bad news, in addition to the breach, is that it turns out that the third-party vendor managing the data had a flawed history when it comes to managing customer data.

The first question such a board committee might ask is, "Why didn't we know this about the vendor?" The next question might be, "Who made the decision to use that vendor?" No chief information security officer or chief risk officer, or any executive serving in that line of authority, including the general counsel, wants to be called into the next meeting of the risk committee.

How will the third party be required to make demonstrations of proof, in writing, as to the assessment of the risk posed by the aforementioned operational environment? Every nation has complementary risks as well as unique risks. It is important to understand these distinctions when making decisions about the use of third-party vendors.

Vendors can be slow, uncooperative, and even recalcitrant in providing information regarding a cyber breach. Without accurate, timely information from vendors, companies cannot make reasonable judgments relative to the operational risk profile. There is no meaningful management of risk without vendor commitment to accountability.

Historically, vendors have had superior positioning by using vendor agreements, such as the master service agreements and service level agreements, for example. Vendor agreements will also favor vendors. While some vendors are not open to negotiation, others are. Even if vendors won't budge on terms, it is critical, from a cyber risk management perspective, to put the terms on the table for negotiation. It is important to be able to demonstrate, in writing, that attempts were made to negotiate terms essential to managing cyber risk. If the vendor won't agree, a decision has to be made about whether to move forward with the agreement. Either way, you will have at least addressed the issue. Managing cyber risk isn't always about getting your way. It's about making decisions that have the potential to imperil the organization or protect it.

8. **Assign a vendor accountability executive.** Get every vendor to designate a single person (who has solid knowledge of the vendor controls) who will work with you and who will have the obligation to convey any information necessary to ongoing cyber risk management. This is important because oftentimes information of value gets siloed or, for whatever reason, doesn't get properly conveyed. While it may be easy to establish this requirement with new vendors, it may be more difficult with existing vendors until contract renewal. Additionally, as part of the planning process, negotiate meeting quarterly with the vendor. Of course, this is not always necessary, but it is for higher-risk vendors. Meetings may be in-person or held as conference calls, subject to preference, venue, and availability. In the event of a Severity-1 breach, the meetings should be held in person when possible unless extraordinary circumstances prevent it.

If the vendor chronically fails to produce desired documentation, for example, an on-site meeting should be pursued. There should be a formal accounting of the meeting, always in writing. The accountable vendor executive and your cyber risk executive should follow up on all open issues. The meetings are essential for managing issues and outcomes, and having them also conveys the message that you mean business. If you treat the cyber breach lightly, delay responding, and/or don't show up on site, vendors may get the idea that you aren't taking the breach seriously—which may lead them to take it less seriously as well. On-site meetings with vendors are viewed positively by regulators and are consistent with evolving regulatory expectations and insurers.

9. **Initiate a master service agreement.** The MSA should be issued by the client company, whenever feasible. While this is not always acceptable to vendors, it very often is. Having a vendor issue the MSA often provides the vendor with an advantage. Among other specifics required for inclusion into the MSA, you should specifically designate what the vendor should do in the event of a cyber breach. The vendor often defines what must be done post–cyber breach. That isn't likely to favor your organization. Consider negotiating into the agreement language that addresses the following:

- **Define losses.** Losses should be defined as all losses, liabilities, damages, and claims and all related costs and expenses (including reasonable legal fees and disbursements and costs of forensic investigation, litigation, settlement, judgment, interest, and penalties). In the event of a cyber breach, negotiate that the defined losses should be covered by the vendor. This includes legal and breach investigative costs.

- **Security breach response.** A lot of companies make a mistake here. You want to be notified by the vendor immediately but not more than 24 hours after the identification of the suspected cyber security incident. Establish that any suspected breach involving a security violation is rated as a Severity-1 event. Any Severity-1 incident requires the vendor, at its own cost and to be initiated immediately, to conduct a root cause analysis of the incident. The root cause analysis procedure should be conducted under the jurisdiction of the office of the general counsel in order to establish and maintain attorney-client privilege with respect to all incident work product. Progress reports of the root cause analysis must be provided on a regular basis. You determine what constitutes "a regular basis." It is recommended that a formal call and readout of the findings be convened daily between the vendor and the customer. The vendor must, at the conclusion of the root cause analysis procedure, present its findings and conclusions, as well as its remediation plan.

Require that the report from the vendor should be written for a diverse audience of interested constituents, including management, internal and external legal counsel, corporate customers, and various state and federal regulators, as appropriate. The reason to specify this in any agreement is that some vendors may present only a technical definition of the cyber attack and resulting losses. The greater the definition of the required documentation from vendors, the more useful the reports. The reporting from the vendor must enable you to adequately define the cyber event and the measures needed to manage and remediate the conditions contributing to the cyber breach. The reporting from the vendor should include the following required elements:

- Executive summary for management.
- Technical summary.
- Description of the intrusion or incident.
- Date(s) of intrusion or incident.
- Description of compromised data.
- Description of preliminary mitigation.
- Define the characteristics of the breach condition.
- Define forensic investigation requirements.
- Oversee forensic examination of devices.
- A description of the technical environment impacted.
- Presentation of a preliminary risk management and mitigation strategy.
- Presentation of applicable vendor insurance policies.
- Establish evidentiary chain of custody regarding breached devices.
- Presentation of results of vulnerability scans on specified devices.
- Presentation of vendor status in monitoring the status of any compromised information to determine if illicit use in the gray market had been commenced.
- Presentation of strategy to monitor the web for any continuing and future brand compromise.

CLOUDS FILL THE HORIZON

Embraced as a critical growth strategy by leading U.S. and foreign companies, cloud computing makes a compelling argument in the global economy. The attraction of cloud computing is that companies can expand operations using someone else's technology and at a fraction of the cost of purchasing new technology. Even President Obama is aware of the benefits of migrating electronic medical records into a cloud computing environment as one method of containing out-of-control health care costs. The future of cloud computing seems clear. But does it introduce a different set of risks? A number of emerging risk issues around cloud computing are building like a global storm front. In fact, a 2011 survey conducted by cloud computing vendor

IBM indicated that 77 percent of respondents were concerned that cloud computing would increase privacy risk.

Clouds are emerging from virtually every geography, and if clouds currently do not exist in a geography, it seems certain that they will in the next few years. There's a lot at stake; clouds represent a lot of growth and a lot of revenue. Reflecting on the value of the cloud market, the press for market share is already here, and there are diplomatic, political, as well as economic issues in the mix. For example, cloud providers in the European Union charge that cloud providers in the United States should not be used by EU companies. The allegation? That the Uniting and Strengthening America by Providing Appropriate Tools Required to Intercept and Obstruct Terrorism, otherwise known as the USA Patriot Act, gives the United States easy access to personal information stored in U.S. cloud providers. Of course, other nations have low barriers to access to acquire sensitive personal information as well, especially when such information is relative to national security.

It is reasonable to think of clouds as the third-party vendors of the future, where a new generation of providers based in developing nations offer financially competitive storage and data management models. However, there are issues to think about from a cyber risk perspective, and these are questions that must be asked now and in the future. Some of these questions include:

- Who are the owners of the cloud computing organization?
- Are governments with contrary interests involved?
- What is the level of organized crime in that host nation?
- What are the local privacy and data breach laws and regulations?
- What is the level of corruption as evidenced in the Transparency International Corruption Index?
- Is insurance applicable when data is in certain offshore clouds?
- Will it be more difficult to manage and monitor agreement compliance?
- How often should offshore cloud sites be visited and tested for compliance?
- Does the cloud entity use virtual currency? If so, what protections are in place to limit exposure to transnational criminal enterprises?
- Would a cyber war increase information risk because of the geographic location of the cloud operation?
- Would data be more susceptible to a terrorist threat because of its location in a cloud environment in another nation?
- How are background investigations conducted on cloud employees?

This list can be extensive and should reflect the comprehensive questions posed during due diligence of traditional third-party vendors.

Ten top security and privacy executives at an investment conference in New York City were asked this question, "Would you place regulated customer data in the cloud, even if it was encrypted?" One executive from a Japanese firm was the only one who answered that sensitive information would be placed in the cloud. Every other executive answered no, even if the data was encrypted. Their reasoning was simple: No one really knows what level of encryption can be compromised by a government dedicated to breaking it. Data collected over the course of a specified period may not be breakable at the time during which it was acquired. But eventually the data may be broken, and that was a risk the nine security and privacy executives were not willing to accept. The benefit of clouds, in this case, was not worth the risk.

In fairness, though, it must be noted that all third-party vendors, including clouds, are not equal. Some companies will improve their cyber risk exposure by using external vendors, again, including clouds. Why? Because these external organizations will have cyber risk management controls that will prove superior to the client company. Cyber security is expensive, and many companies are not willing or able to invest in the protective mechanisms offered by third-party providers.

Dr. Lothar Determan, a privacy attorney in the Palo Alto, California, office of Baker & McKenzie, writes, "Whether personal data is safer on a system secured by the data controller 'in-house' or on an external vendor depends on security measures deployed by each particular organization. Moving data to the cloud can be a bad thing for data security if the vendor is weak on security and careless. It can be a good thing if the vendor brings better technologies to the table and helps the data controller manage access, data retention and data integrity. And it can be neutral if the vendor's cloud system is more secure, but the way the customer uses the system keeps exposing the data (e.g., because the customer does not configure security to properly restrict data to the appropriate users, the customer uses unsecured connections or the customer downloads data from the cloud to unsecured local devices)."[3]

No one should be under the illusion that such negotiations with traditional third-party or cloud vendors are going to be easy. Some will prove to be productive; others not. But the key consideration is that these negotiations are fundamental to more effectively negotiating agreements that will assist in managing the risks associated with cyber attacks. It is also worth restating that obtaining approvals from vendors is not the only goal. Vendors will give on some issues, and not on others. A lot of factors will be under consideration by vendors. The other goal is to at least attempt to negotiate key elements of the agreements, document all such attempts, and clearly illustrate that all elements of managing cyber risk were addressed. It may not be feasible to change every agreement to your advantage, but it is possible to include in the discussions and negotiations all of the elements pursuant to cyber risk. In the event of a cyber event, you will at least have the documentation needed to defend your prior courses of action and orient the outcome to the extent possible under the restrictions associated with the agreements in place. This alone, deflecting risk, is worth the effort.

A number of risk-related executives have asked the question, "If we know the vendor isn't going to budge, why try to negotiate the point?" The answer is this: You want to be able to demonstrate to the board, to insurers, and to any other interested parties, that the issue was addressed, that the vendor remained unmovable on the point, but that you pushed that agenda. In the confusion and energy that accompany a cyber breach, it is easy to lay blame and to point fingers at who may be at fault. Judgments will likely be made that will linger, as doubt will grow as to whether the correct decisions were made and the appropriate level of due diligence was applied to the vendor that is now associated with the breach. The aftermath of the cyber breach will carry threads of doubt that were raised early on during that stage of confusion. It is important to demonstrate, through the offering of documentation, not only what the vendor was required to do, but also what the vendor had not agreed to do but which you had firmly recommended. Or sometimes failures in negotiation are indications that it is time to move on to another vendor.

 ## NOTES

1. U.S. Department of Health and Human Services, www.hhs.gov/news.
2. Federal Deposit Insurance Corporation, www.fdic.gov.
3. Dr. Lothar Determan, "Data Privacy in the Cloud: A Dozen Myths and Facts," *Privacy Laws and Business*, Issue 121, February 2013.

CHAPTER TEN

Creating Executive Cyber Risk Councils

It takes 20 years to build a reputation and five
minutes to ruin it. If you think about that, you'll do
things differently.

—*Warren Buffett*

T HE SPACE race in the United States accelerated in 1961 when on
May 25 President John F. Kennedy stood before Congress and said,
"This nation should commit itself to achieving the goal, before the
decade is out, of landing a man on the moon and returning him safely to the
earth." This was in response to the threat of Soviet dominance in space. History
was made on July 20, 1969, when *Apollo* 11 landed on the moon and
Neil Armstrong's boot touched the lunar surface. It was thrilling. It was
extraordinarily memorable.

In the history of space exploration, there is another perhaps equally well-
known event: *Apollo* 13. In 1970 *Apollo* 13 was on its way to the moon when
it encountered a high-risk incident, an explosion aboard the spacecraft,
forcing the cancellation of the plan to again land on the moon and prompting
a return to Earth. There were no guarantees the crippled ship would get the

crew back home alive. But thanks to the mission control team at NASA and the grit of the *Apollo* 13 astronauts, Apollo was a successful failure—the mission of going to the moon failed, but they made it back and no one was killed. Mission control was confronted with an extraordinary, complex predicament. This was not something anyone expected. They didn't plan for it. There wasn't a Plan B. Nothing in the brief history of space exploration had prepared anyone for this event.

Similarities exist between *Apollo* 13 and cyber attacks. For one thing, cyber attacks are, in the history of business, relatively new. There was a time not too long ago when cyber attacks were unthinkable. How could there be such an attack when the only computers were mainframes the size of a large room? The only distributed data was on paper, in files, in different locations.

Things go wrong when there's a cyber attack. But as former NASA flight director Gene Kranz once said, failure is not an option. Failure is not an option when it comes to managing risk, either. The stakes are too high. It may seem poor form to suggest that a cyber attack may be as critical as an accident aboard a spacecraft carrying human beings. But cyber attacks have the potential to be devastating.

NASA's mission control is an interesting model, perhaps even for managing risk and developing an executive risk council. There were various kinds of engineers on the team, plus medical personnel, physicists, technical communications specialists, media specialists, executive management, third-party vendors, and so on. Nothing stressed the model more than Apollo 13. Nothing may stress a corporation like a critical cyber attack. The outcomes are never certain, the risk of failure ever present, the reality often veiled by layers of complexity.

Executive risk councils have a vital function in today's environment, just as mission control had a vital function during the space race and beyond. Cyber attacks are marked by increasing frequency, intensity, and risk impact. And no entity is immune. Companies large and small are targeted by nation-states, organized crime, and cyber attackers associated with protests of a dizzying array of social and political causes. Like the Internet, Web, social media, and mobile devices, the cyber threat has left little untouched in this world.

But there are effective ways to combat cyber attacks!

One of the mistakes made in the somewhat brief history of cyber space is viewing cyber attacks as a technology security issue. While it is true that both technology and security play a major role in cyber attacks, to view the attacks as exclusively in the domain of electrons isn't based on reality. Cyber attacks involve people. So do the methods of managing the risks associated with them.

Cyber criminals are smart. For them, stealing information is a business. They target companies, looking for rich archives of personal and business information. Large companies, medium-size companies, and even small companies are targeted. Not only are cyber criminals looking for information, but, like a burglar, they are looking for information that is not well protected. If there are two homes, and inside each home there is an equal amount of money to steal but one home is locked down and secure, the thief will likely move to the home with less security.

Criminals often look for the path of least resistance. They're not necessarily lazy. They're just pursuing intelligent paths. Companies need to be smart to manage the risks associated with cyber attacks. This is not a one-person job. Managing these risks requires a more broadly distributed perspective. Managing these risks is multidimensional.

Curiously, the word "cyber" often fails to ring any alarms. Companies often say, "Why would anyone target us?" This is what they say before the breach. The Internet and the Web have become the great democratizers of marketing, with the Davids of the world assuming the corporate persona of a Goliath. Using the tools of the digital age, a one-person company can look as sophisticated and global as, well, a sophisticated and global company.

Trust and reputation are irrevocably linked. Violate the trust, compromise the reputation. Fair or unfair, this is reality. Reputation is arguably any company's most valuable asset. A breached company is not usually a bad company. A breach doesn't mean that the people in the company are bad. But sometimes that is what hackers want you to believe. Without trust, the information that is the fuel of the economic engine of commerce that sustains employment and tax revenue for government becomes a legal, financial, regulatory, and reputation liability with potential negative impact. Translation: loss of market share, market preference, and dominance; loss of shareholder and stakeholder value; and loss of investor confidence, which may even result in the loss of geopolitical positioning and diplomatic power. Trust is at the heart of reputation. Once trust is lost, it is hard to regain. That's why it is essential for the attackers to go for the reputational jugular—trust.

Trust is a most human characteristic. It is not something automatically conferred or at least it shouldn't be. Trust should be earned. Enterprise trust is not really any different from fundamental human trust. But enterprise trust has a lot of moving parts, a number of components that are managed by many people. Each one has a role, a purpose, and a level of trust.

Cyber attack impact is variable—and assured. Fail to adequately safeguard information and the pain is quickly felt: regulatory scrutiny, fines, civil and even criminal litigation, loss of market value, loss of customer base, loss of market dominance, loss of reputation, and on and on. The list is long, and can be costly. Unregulated intellectual property and trade secret compromise can have similar—and perhaps even greater—impact.

So what to do about it? Establishing an executive risk council can have a substantial impact on any organization. While an executive risk council is not the silver bullet of cyber defense (there is no silver bullet), it can provide significant value to almost any organization.

Some companies have begun to evolve in terms of managing risk, but many have not. The U.S. regulators for the financial services industry have played a role in shaping this vision. Few companies appreciate regulators. But regulators are increasingly placing an emphasis on top management and boards getting educated on cyber risk. This is absolutely critical because this is where budgets come from, and where reputations are often shaped. Intelligent and lucid boards of directors and top management shape culture and lay the foundation for how their companies should operate. Placing an emphasis on the management and board getting cyber smart pays dividends. One of the things it accomplishes is raising the level of awareness across the company about the cyber risk.

This causes various areas of an enterprise to examine operational risk and the threat of a cyber attack and its potential impact. It can lead to a discussion of how to mitigate the risk, which can in turn lead to an examination of the different people in an organization who have something to contribute to that defense.

First, it should be noted that every employee is part of the fabric of a cyber defense. But there are some who must be part of the management defense—the guards at the gates, so to speak. Bringing together the right team is essential in managing risk.

An executive cyber risk council brings together the right parties needed to define the problem and the solution, and then manage the process, and then make adjustments to the program as needed as things change. For too long, security has been perceived as either an issue of guards, gates, and guns, or as an IT issue. Even today, across many companies, risk is perceived as a technology issue or a security issue, and the assumption is that the answer to managing that risk resides within the domains of technology and security. Nothing could be further from the truth. This kind of thinking can get even the most reputation-conscious companies in deep trouble, and quickly. The reality is that managing risk is all of these things and more, and should be reflected in the composition of the executive cyber risk council.

THE GOAL OF THE EXECUTIVE CYBER RISK COUNCIL

The goal of an executive cyber risk council is to reduce to the lowest degree possible the impact of a breach, or to prevent a breach if possible. The council needs to understand the fundamentals of cyber threats, and how to defend against legal, financial, regulatory, and reputation risk. This includes recognizing potential risk impact and working to control it. It forces the team to confront potential loss associated with a cyber breach.

An important function of the executive cyber risk council is to look forward with respect to changing conditions in threat and risk conditions, thinking holistically about cyber risk issues, and then acting aggressively to manage the risk. So on the one hand, the executive cyber risk council is something of a study group, but it is also a planning, action, and response organization.

An executive risk council is no silver bullet against hackers, internal or external, but it is a good starting point for building awareness where it counts—the CEO and the board.

The participants of the executive cyber risk council may vary by size of organization, industry sector, and so on. But the mission serves not only to manage the risk condition, but to manage expectation and commitment. Having a functional, actively engaged, and highly visible executive cyber risk council sets an example, makes a statement. This statement of commitment is important to regulators, business partners, investors, and insurers. The existence of the executive risk cyber council says that the entity is aware of the threat dimension, the likelihood of attack, the fact that real damage can result from an attack, and that it is committed to defending the integrity of its information or its customers' information.

Warren Buffett's quote comes to mind: "It takes 20 years to build a reputation and 5 minutes to ruin it. If you think about that, you'll do things differently." It hardly seems fair. But so much in life isn't fair. Think about it from a customer's point of view. It doesn't matter if the customer is a lone consumer or a giant corporation or government agency. Most people want to do business with organizations that have a good reputation. The reasons are obvious. Do business where there's trouble and you're likely to get trouble in return. Managing risk by managing reputation is a rational approach to managing business.

All companies targeted by cyber attacks face one great commonality: the potential compromise of reputation—reputation risk. The best advice is to always think postbreach and act prebreach. An executive cyber risk council should serve the function of thinking from a postbreach perspective. If a breach occurred, what would the company do? How would each member of the council react? What would be their function? How would they work together? What would they tell employees? What would they say to the media and to business partners? How would they stop the breach? How would they investigate it? Who should contact law enforcement? Which law enforcement agency should be contacted, and when? What about getting the regulators involved? Which ones? When?

An effective executive cyber risk council can address these and other questions before a strike occurs, helping to reduce the impact of a potentially devastating cyber attack, and maintain that ever important bond of trust, which defines reputation. While an executive risk council may sound like a fairly straightforward approach to helping manage risk, the composition of such a council may not be so readily obvious.

WHO SHOULD BE INCLUDED IN THE EXECUTIVE RISK COUNCIL?

Look at the impact of a breach and it becomes increasingly obvious who should be involved in an executive risk council. Although companies and situations vary, here is an outline of who should be included:

- **Legal officer.** The breach impact footprint is large. A breach first and foremost becomes a legal issue. The legal challenge involves regulatory considerations, breach of contracts, civil litigation, and even criminal prosecution in some cases. Fundamental to effective risk management in the case of an information breach of any kind is the attorney-client privilege. So it is vital to include a legal representative. For smaller companies, especially those without in-house counsel, consider working with an external legal resource, one with knowledge of information management and risk. But make no mistake: A cyber attack can and will have legal consequences.

  In some cases, smaller companies have sought the advice of general-practice attorneys who lack experience in cyber breaches and the resulting risk. In a recent case, for example, a smaller company used its legal counsel to handle the termination of an employee accused of information theft. Without getting into the specifics of the case, the legal counsel provided advice to the client that conflicted with the law enforcement efforts to apprehend the criminal. An attorney with law enforcement experience and information theft experience would likely have provided better advice and counsel, resulting in a better conclusion to the case. The company did not have the satisfaction of seeing the justice system work to its maximum potential, and the criminal is likely working elsewhere, perpetrating another fraud. So getting the right legal counsel can have a major impact.

Placing a knowledgeable and experienced attorney with privacy, data protection, and law enforcement experience on the team can be invaluable.

■ **Risk officer.** Some companies have a chief risk officer. For a variety of reasons, many do not. Budget is sometimes a reason not to have one. Others don't believe it is necessary to have a chief risk officer. Still others believe that if the company is not regulated there is no reason to have such a position. But a chief risk officer role is critical, regardless of the business size, industry sector, and global reach. Even if the company doesn't have a formal title of chief risk officer, someone should be appointed to that role, even if it is not a full-time endeavor. The importance of it is that someone should sit outside of technology and security in order to look at a broader range of factors that could result in a risk event and be able to orchestrate prevention as well as postbreach activities. In some cases it may be a legal officer, in others the chief financial officer. Make sure that risk officer is a critical part of the executive risk council. Having someone who is continuously analyzing risk and its potential impact is vital to any organization. Even some small and midsize companies, especially in financial services, are creating chief risk officer positions. Every breach results in a cost to the company, and that is why it is also important to have the CFO on the council, because that officer can be influential in making budget available for preventive measures. As has been stated elsewhere in this book, it is almost always less costly to prevent a breach than deal with the aftermath of one—and there's a lot less certainty around final outcomes when a breach occurs.

■ **Security.** A chief security officer (CSO) and/or chief information security officer (CISO) is a natural for the executive risk council, right? This is an obvious role, perhaps, but not entirely so. As odd as it may seem, companies often get this one wrong. In larger operations there may be both a CSO and a CISO. In most companies, though, and especially in smaller to midsize ones, the CISO is the representative on the executive risk council. But this can be problematic. Some CISOs are well versed in physical security, some are not. Having a physical security specialist on the executive risk council is critical. The reason is that some breaches occur as a result of gaps between physical and logical security. One of the main reasons that companies often fail physical perimeter stress testing is that a CISO without adequate physical security training and experience designed the mechanisms that are intended to prevent unauthorized access. This often means that gaps in the defense are present. These gaps are often identifiable through even light surveillance of physical access points at the target facility.

Here's an example. Unless the CISO has adequate physical security awareness, it may be quite possible for intruders to use social engineering tactics to gain access into the building under false circumstances. This is important, because once inside, there is an assumption that whoever is present is supposed to be there. Understanding of zone security, social engineering, and training of employees on this point is fundamental to protecting information. So having this role on the executive cyber risk council is a must.

Information security must contain three very specific characteristics: (1) physical security, (2) technical or logical security, and (3) administrative security. The regulators make reference to these aspects of security, and each should have equal measure. In many companies, there is a wide gulf between physical security and technical and administrative security. This is a weakness that increases the likelihood of breach success, particularly when an intrusion involves physical penetration of the target company.

▪ **IT infrastructure.** Technology infrastructure is vital to the council because most every activity the company engages in involves a computer, a tablet, a smartphone, the network, the Internet, and servers. IT touches everything. A chief technology officer (CTO) or director of information technology is a good candidate for this role on the executive cyber risk council. Too often, the technologists help select the technology based on its performance and its "cool" effect. This is something of an Achilles' heel of the technical enterprise. Not only do a lot of technical people feel the pull to bring new technology into the workplace, but a lot of other executives do as well.

Having a technology officer on the executive cyber risk council accomplishes two things. First, it brings to a seat at the table someone who understands the power of technology. Second, it is something of an early warning system that the company is looking at new technology for consideration and deployment. On many occasions the security and risk team gets blindsided when new technology is introduced. For example, the information security team will sometimes be told that, say, tablets are being purchased for the board of directors because they want one. "Oh, and those tablets will be arriving tomorrow. Make sure they're secure." The executive cyber risk council is a forum for getting insight and perspective on what going on at all levels of the company, and the technologist on it can be a great asset to understanding the technological advantages of a product or system.

- **Information and records management/chief information officer.** While many organizations are transitioning to paperless records, many are not. Most environments currently are a mix of paper and electronic records. This magnifies the risk. For companies that are going to maintain this dual-data structure, equal protection should be given to both formats. A Social Security number written on a piece of paper is equally vulnerable to the same number contained in a storage device or computer. In fact, sometimes the piece of paper is even more vulnerable to compromise because of so much emphasis on electronic data. It's also good to note that many regulations specify both paper and electronic records. Include the chief information officer (CIO) or records management executive in the council.

- **Business continuity planning/disaster recovery.** Business continuity planning and disaster recovery are critical to the executive risk council. The larger the global footprint, the greater the potential risk impact, and the greater the likelihood of an event. A cyber attack against the weakest link in a company's supply chain creates substantial impact. An attack against the local utility grid may be equally damaging. BCP/DR contributions to the executive cyber risk council should include issues such as workplace violence, terrorist attack, war, cyber attacks, natural disasters, extreme weather events, utility outages, and other factors that may imperil the enterprise. The absence of this representation on the council may result in increased risk impact.

- **Marketing and sales.** Though they are often not included in executive risk councils, it is important to remember that marketing and sales executives are intimately related to the company's reputation, and this part of the workforce is often directly impacted first. In the event of a breach, it is necessary to address this issue with customers, and having a senior representative on the executive cyber risk council will provide the executive risk council with better perspective. Their participation can also provide insight into customer expectations and concerns.

- **Human resources.** Get the entire employee base on board with the security message. HR is often the organization that has the greatest reach to all employees, from onboarding to exit interviews. HR needs to be part of the solution to risk impact management and prevention. One of the biggest problems around security is lack of awareness among the employee population. On the executive cyber risk council, HR can serve as a view into how the organization can be educated on the issue of risk, coordinating this effort with the risk management and security executives, and helping to design a program that contains the right messaging with the right delivery model.

■ **Information privacy.** Not every company has a chief privacy officer (CPO), though many do. If there is no CPO in the organization, there should at least be someone who is charged with the responsibility of managing information privacy. Make sure someone is responsible for ascertaining that information privacy is understood and that the associated policies are in place. Also, remember that privacy includes not only personal information, such as financial and medical information, but also intellectual property and trade secrets. Having this employee on the executive cyber risk council is important because it will give the council perspective on the type of information at risk and its sensitivity.

■ **Internal audit.** A representative from internal audit will add substantial value, making certain that the internal audit plan embraces the full dimensions of the scope and risk. Also, it has direct linkage to the audit committee of the board of directors. Increasingly, auditors are becoming part of the risk management perspective, though not necessarily part of the risk management team due to their need to remain independent. As part of the executive cyber risk council, the internal auditor is able to apprise the council on a continuing basis on the status of ongoing regulatory and other concerns pursuant to security and risk.

■ **Corporate communications.** Developing a media response plan before a breach is fundamental and should be part of every company's corporate governance initiative. If perception is reality, then perception should not be left for others to define, lest that become the reality. The communications executive on the executive cyber risk council will be able to place into perspective the many factors that influence a breach, and participate in ongoing discussions about the internal and external conditions of the organization and its threat environment. Breaches can be complicated. The ability to communicate knowledgeably and effectively has great value. And let's face it, when it comes to dealing with the media, many executives lack expertise. The communications executive can also be a media coach to the council.

- **Alliance management.** Strategic alliance and joint venture partner relationships are at risk in the event of a breach. The alliance partner may have a great deal to lose, from a capital investment to its reputation. Placing someone with a trusted relationship with the partner will be an advantage when a breach comes. Having an alliance management executive participate in the council allows for proper messaging (working with corporate communications) to the various companies who may have skin (and risk) in the breach.

- **Regulatory compliance.** A regulatory compliance representative is critical, particularly if the breach involves personally identifiable information (PII) or personal health information (PHI). Depending on the size of the company, compliance may be part of the legal office, so the legal representative may fill this position. If not, someone from compliance will be able to convey to the council the regulatory requirements associated with managing data and what to do in the event of a breach.

- **Vendor management.** When a breach occurs, it is likely the breach may come through a third-party vendor. Having an executive risk council member with a relationship with the external vendor can save time and money. Just as it is likely that a breach will originate with the external vendor managing its customer's information, it is equally likely that the external vendor may be uncooperative in the event of a breach at its facility. Depending on the size of the company and the number of external vendors, consider rotating members in vendor management. Alternatively, seek cooperation from the most senior executive of the vendor management committee for participation in the council.

- **Executive sponsor.** The more senior the title, the better. For smaller organizations, it may be the CEO. But whether it is the director of internal audit, the general counsel, or the CFO, the executive sponsor must have direct access to the board and to the executive management team. This is invaluable for budgetary approvals. A council member will have a strong understanding of the need to prevent breaches and reduce the impact of one. Having an executive sponsor will keep the key risk-related issues in front of the top management and the board of directors. The importance of keeping these issues in front of the board cannot be emphasized too much. In fact, for financial institutions, this is a requirement. So the executive sponsor must be responsive to the council and represent its concerns, and must obtain the correct level of funding in order to effectively manage the organization's risk.

■ **Independent adviser.** An outside opinion is always advisable. Bringing in an independent third party has the advantage of providing a perspective that is not influenced by corporate politics or trying to impress the boss with showboating. An independent adviser can contribute information and analysis critical to the formulation of decisions, often providing insight that is not available from inside the enterprise. Organizations have cultures. Cultures are often shaped by policies, a way of doing things. Policies can also be shaped by culture. In either case, there is an internal dynamic. That dynamic may be right or wrong; it is just the way things are done.

Here's an example: The company in question was global in its reach, but its risk assessment approach was very narrow, focusing only on the threats defined by its own staff. The staff, for whatever reason, thought about threats only from their own experience base. They looked at every threat from a U.S. point of view. Never did they consider assessing threats at the foreign-country level. This approach left them vulnerable, unable to reasonably foresee the developing threat conditions in the other countries where they operated. Unable to foresee such threats, they had no defenses with which to counter the threats and no strategy for managing the risks emanating from those threats. It's not that the company was defenseless; it wasn't. But its risk management program lacked a fully dimensioned view, which could result in an unsatisfactory result. That unsatisfactory result often translates into an impaired reputation.

The perspective of an independent party has significant value. It doesn't mean that the independent adviser has to be at every meeting. But quarterly meetings are a good idea because things change quickly and often. If nothing else, having that independent adviser should bring to the executive cyber risk council the satisfaction of knowing that it is exploring various elements of ongoing threats and the potential risk from someone who is less likely to say something because it is the safe or appropriate thing to say.

As Henry Ford remarked, "You can't build a reputation on what you are going to do." But you can build a reputation, and maintain it, by how risk is managed. Building an effective executive cyber risk council, and maintaining it for the long term, is the best way to keep perspective and to holistically understand the many vectors from which the unexpected may come. There is an order-of-magnitude difference between the unexpected and the unanticipated.

A cyber attack may be unexpected, but it should never be unanticipated. Managing risk requires anticipating the threat, as well as how to manage the risk arising from it. One of the best methods for anticipating the full range of cyber complications springing from the cyber threat is through the executive cyber risk council. Every member has a voice. Every member has a perspective—and a responsibility. And every member has a vested interest in the outcome. The problem is vastly more complex than any one individual, and so is the solution to managing outcomes. Everyone should have a compelling interest in countering the many varied types of cyber attacks. Forming an executive cyber risk council will help focus thinking about the problem and developing in-depth countermeasures to maintain information integrity in an increasingly intense cyber threat environment.

CHAPTER ELEVEN

Early Warnings

Something Bad Is on the Way

One thorn of experience is worth a whole wilderness of warning.

—James Russell Lowell

EARLY WARNINGS come in a variety of expressions. Some warnings are technical signals; others are behavioral. The quote by poet and diplomat James Russell Lowell is dead-on accurate. History really is one of the best early warning indicators: The pain emanating from that "thorn of experience" is telling.

Perhaps the best early warning system is the media. Looking online or reading newspapers the old-fashioned way provides clear evidence that the cyber attack problem is worsening and is not likely to improve in the near future. Even though only a minority of cyber breaches are reported in the media, the numbers are compelling and the impact is often substantial, even devastating. Expecting a cyber attack is an appropriate posture.

There are a number of early warnings that can signal a problem. These aren't the computer that's running slowly because it may be infected with a virus. There are a few early warning signals that companies often ignore or are simply unaware of their significance.

It is no secret that some of the better-protected companies are those that have felt the pain of a prior breach. Depending on a number of conditions associated with the company and its attackers, that pain may have been significant, resulting in legal, regulatory, financial, and reputation risk impact. With an average data breach cost of more than $7 million, according to the Ponemon Institute, the financial hit can be especially painful. Many breaches cost far, far more. Given the mega breaches of late 2013 and 2014, there's no telling what the total breach cost will turn out to be for the affected parties. One thing is certain, though: The value of reputation is immeasurable. The sooner an attack is identified, the better.

Not all companies that have experienced data breaches have listened well to the voice of experience within their own walls, but they should have. Many companies have reported multiple breaches. So either those companies failed to learn from their experience, or the cyber attackers were ingenious. Maybe both considerations can be true simultaneously. As history will clearly illustrate to anyone willing to examine it, data breaches, like the stingray, have a long tail that can deliver a painful strike and a memorable legacy, none of it good. For many companies, the process of responding to a data breach is very distracting. It sidetracks a company from the primary mission and necessarily switches it to a subsidiary mission—managing the event. That is why those that have been attacked generally have no interest in a repeat performance.

Curiously, some organizations have been the target of numerous breaches, yet they never really progressed to the point where trying to prevent them was important enough. History wasn't much of an early warning. In these circumstances, there are a number of factors that come into play:

- The company doesn't have the money to invest more in managing operational risk, the result of narrow profit margins, higher costs of doing business, a beleaguered economy, or other financial issues.
- The board and the senior management team have accepted breaches as a cost of doing business and have made a conscious or unconscious decision to roll the dice and roll with the punches, as they assuredly will come.
- The board and senior management lack awareness. This sounds improbable given a breach history. But often these executives fail to connect the dots regarding security, risk, privacy, regulatory compliance, and data breaches.
- Some board members and senior executives perceive that data breaches are applicable only to personal information and not to business proprietary information such as intellectual property and trade secrets.

- There is also a lack of awareness about what hackers can do over the Internet, ranging from various types of denials of service to Web-based financial scams and frauds.
- Many lack awareness of nation-state espionage and transnational organized crime networks.
- Although it seems unlikely given the history of cyber attacks, many executives simply do not believe that they will be targeted. "We're too small to be noticed." "No one knows we even exist." "We don't have anything anyone else would want." "We couldn't stop these attacks if we wanted to."
- Many companies remain unaware of regulatory data protection and reporting requirements. The executives in these companies simply fail to do what the statutes and regulations say they must do. Overall, compliance with such statutes and regulations is relatively low, with one highly regulated state estimating that compliance percentage is in the single digits.

For these reasons and others known only to those inside some enterprises, early warnings, at least in the form of historical precedent, remain unacknowledged or ignored. But there are other early warning signals.

 ## TECHNICAL SIGNALS ARE THERE—BUT YOU'VE GOT TO LOOK

Internet protocol (IP) addresses are unique numbers that identify any device connecting to the Internet. This includes computers, tablets, even printers and copiers. DARPA, the Defense Advanced Research Projects Agency, one of the developers of the Internet, defined an IP address this way: "A name indicates what we seek. An address indicates where it is. A route indicates how to get there."

Depending on the type of business, many companies have several kinds of IP addresses in the enterprise. Let's face it, a business today without any IP addresses is a dead business. But IP addresses are not either a one or a zero, or black and white. Many executives don't even know what an IP address means or what the "I" and the "P" stand for. Literally! This is often reflective of the gap between the more senior management team, security, and the technology people. Not knowing what kind of IP addresses are in the environment, though, quickly becomes a management concern.

Among IP addresses, there are authorized IP addresses and unauthorized IP addresses. The former is one way in which much business is conducted. The latter is how businesses are quite often breached.

Legitimate IP addresses make the wheels of commerce turn. The problem is that it is not always easy to make distinctions between what is a legitimate IP address and what is an IP address of hostile intent. It isn't so much that this process is extremely difficult. It's just that going through the exercise is another process to add to an already burdensome list of things to do. But there's also another concern.

A company was under attack. The cyber assault turned out to be significant, its origins offshore. In fact, upon examining the range of IP addresses, it turned out the attacks were originating from multiple locations in Eastern Europe and several cities in China. The IP addresses were associated with transnational organized criminal operations and the usual range of criminal pursuits, from human trafficking to narcotics distribution. Knowing that the IP addresses are toxic provides great incentive to mitigate the associated risks—or at least that is how it is supposed to work. But in this case, though, it got a bit more complicated. It seems that some of the toxic IP addresses came not directly from criminals. They came from the victim company's customers, similar to what was discussed in Chapter 2. That targeted company was doing business with customers that had been successfully penetrated by criminals. Doing business with that infected company thereby infected the targeted company, so now there were at least two victims. Ordinarily, the prudent advice and subsequent action would be to block the hostile or toxic IP addresses and notify the other company that it had been targeted. That's what should have been done. But this can often be confusing and is not without some degree of risk of irritating the customer, or so some executives believe.

The targeted company, when advised to notify its corporate customer that it had been compromised, declined to do so. It didn't want to raise such a sensitive issue with a customer. The concern was that the customer company would take offense, that it might overreact and cancel its contract, that its reputation would be tarnished and it would blame the messenger. But this was absolutely the wrong approach to take, and there are several reasons why.

Even if they do blame the messenger, it would be counterproductive for a company to ignore the concern. They are increasing their liability by potentially infecting other organizations. It's like spreading the flu. Most of those exposed are going to contract it, accept it into the enterprise, and suffer the consequences. So telling the customer that they are transmitting toxic IP addresses is important. It helps everyone. It helps them reduce their liability, and it helps their network of companies to avoid getting hit. Chances are, no one in the company is aware of the problem and they are likely to be grateful for the heads-up. The longer the condition goes unrecognized within their organization, the greater their liability.

Also, consider that the customer company that is unknowingly inserting toxic IP addresses into your enterprise may hold it against you if you fail to notify them that they are in possession of toxic IP addresses and spreading them indiscriminately. Failure to notify the customer company may increase your liability!

These toxic IP addresses can be identified before they do too much damage, but someone's got to check. One way is to simply test the environment, determining a specific sample size of IP addresses. Identify all authorized IP addresses, then determine if the unauthorized samples are toxic or benign. If there are unauthorized IP addresses, investigate: Where did those IP addresses come from? If they are authorized, make sure they are not toxic. Work with the IT security team to determine toxicity. It's important to remember that not all authorized IP addresses are benign, and not all unauthorized IP addresses are toxic. But managing risk is much harder without knowing what is in the environment. Unfortunately, too many organizations make assumptions that all of the IP addresses in their environment must be okay. This approach has led to many disappointing results.

Another potential early warning signal is the Internet service provider (ISP). Unfortunately, ISPs are sometimes selected for the wrong reasons: The price was right, the location was right, the terms were right, and so on. But the telling fact is that ISPs are not created equally. Some ISPs fail to monitor traffic responsibly, allowing suspect transmissions that may involve criminal activity. This happens a lot, and it is usually a violation of the ISP's governance and should be a violation of the contracting company's governance. It is important to conduct formal due diligence on ISPs. When a breach occurs, and if it involves an offshore ISP, things may get complicated, the ISP may be less responsive, and the damage associated with the breach may continue to proliferate until cooperation is forced. Many breach investigations have yielded information implicating ISPs, including some in the United States. Look carefully at ISP track records. If the ISP is located in higher-risk, corrupt nations, look twice. If necessary, manage the risk by selecting another ISP.

The important thing to remember is that ISPs are part of any enterprise. What they do and how they do it matters. Make sure that any ISP that is going to become part of the enterprise is fully vetted. Yes, it is an extra step, and yes, it can add to an already burdensome workload, but it is definitely worth the effort.

KNOW WHO'S INSIDE THE ENTERPRISE

This sounds pretty simple, but it is not. Not only is it critical to understand what IP addresses in the environment may be toxic and that responsible ISPs are being engaged, it is also important to understand which employees, as well as the employees of any external vendors, are inside the walls. It is important because, once inside the walls, there's a conveyance of trust.

Here's how that conclusion was made: background investigations. Background investigations can be somewhat like medical examinations, but with one big difference. The physician conducting the physical is (or at least should be) licensed to practice medicine. Conducting background investigations doesn't always require the same degree of expertise and licensing. Depending on a lot of factors, a physical examination can simply amount to a doctor looking at a patient's throat, ears, eyes, and so on, in a process that may take only a few minutes. Alternatively, some physical examinations are intensive and can take more than a day of patient-doctor time, plus the time of technicians, nurses, and other staff. There is also more expanded use of technology to conduct full-body scans, as well as any localized areas of concern. These exams are obviously more detailed, render greater details about the patient's health condition, and of course cost more money. It may also be argued that such an approach has greater value to the patient, to the attending physicians and staff, and to any interested third parties, such as a board of directors that is looking to make certain determinations about, say, hiring a CEO or extending the contract of the current one.

Background investigations are extremely variable, just as medical checkups are, and the results are equally variable. Like the medical physical, background investigations can provide signals or indicators of certain behaviors. The greater the level of detail about a particular illness, the more effective the management of the disorder. The more that is known about the background of an employee, the better the potential for future predictability. Although background checks are not foolproof (and neither are medical physicals), the key concept here is early warning. If there is a financial fraud inside the company, it would be useful to know that, say, one of the employees there, with virtually unrestricted access to certain data, had filed for bankruptcy, was deeply in debt, and had previously been convicted of a financial fraud. While that would not necessarily prove that the employee was part of the fraud, such findings would trigger the need for additional examination of the person's background. At least it's a clue. Knowing such information in advance would potentially result in an early warning indicator, causing a review of certain behaviors and conditions.

Understanding the background of every employee is invaluable. Ensuring that external vendors are doing the same for their employees is equally valuable. Here's an early warning signal that is not always evident but can be if you negotiate it into your service level agreements. It's simply this: If there is a breach in the external vendor's environment, whether or not your data is involved, you need a heads-up. Period. They don't have to disclose confidential information. They don't have to violate anyone's trust. But they do need to let you know if something is going on that could potentially impact your organization. And that's not all.

Make sure that the external provider is obligated to inform you when any of their employees with access to your data appear on the radar screen for additional background investigations or additional drug tests. There have been cases where employees have been under suspicion by their employer, the employer conducts additional background checks and even additional drug tests, yet the employee is still allowed to access sensitive customer data as part of their job. As has been stated so eloquently, "That dog don't hunt!" It's important information to know, and breaches have happened because the external vendor had suspicions about an employee, conducted one or more additional background investigations and drug tests, the findings were inconclusive, the employee was allowed to continue with access to sensitive customer data, and the external vendor's corporate customer was never notified of the suspicion. The next thing you know, there's been a breach.

Yes, there are complications that can occur for the external vendor. Yes, the employee may protest and may threaten legal action. And there is always the chance that the external vendor is wrong about the employee. But here's the thing: The potential risk is huge and costly. It may result in regulatory impairments and civil or even criminal litigation. It may end up being reported in the media, broadcast across the massive social media landscape, resulting in a lot of negative publicity. The bottom line? Companies need to require third-party vendors by contract to agree to this point. If the vendor doesn't agree, and such arrangement is not up for negotiation, then consider another vendor.

There's always pushback on this advice. Companies like to work with the same vendors they've been using for a long time. That's understandable. It can be time-consuming and disruptive to change vendors, no doubt about that. But before rejecting this out of hand, consider this: If there is going to be a data breach in your company, there is a better than reasonable likelihood that the breach will come via a third-party vendor.

Here's another tip. Monitor what employees are actually doing, especially those with access to sensitive data. Web surfing is often monitored, for example. Employees are restricted from, say, visiting pornography sites. Some companies employ e-mail monitoring programs to see what employees are sending out of the enterprise. But there is one area that some companies ignore and that has resulted in data breaches.

In one case, an employee with extensive access had downloaded a number of software licenses that would enable criminals in other countries, for a fee paid to the employee, to steal critical information. So monitoring what employees may be downloading from even legitimate web sites is one way of detecting breach potential. Question: If the company isn't doing business in, say, Finland, why would an employee download a Finnish license for a software program giving someone in Finland access to company computers? Answer: There's no good reason. More than likely, this is an early warning signal. Check into it!

 ## WHAT A WEB WE WEAVE . . . WHEN SURFING

At home during the weekend, the executive was surfing the Web. Typing his name into a search engine, he was, as many do, looking to see what was being said about him. Maybe kudos for a speech he had given, perhaps a snide remark by a competitor, possibly an article in the local newspaper or even one of the national business publications. It was then that he discovered a web site that featured his name and his company's name. He also discovered information about his personal life, finances, and family on another web site, a scam web site in the business of bilking investors. It turns out the scam had been going on for several years, but no one had discovered it.

His discovery prompted the other senior executives in the organization to start their own Web surfing ventures in an effort to see if their boss was the only victim. As it turns out, he was. Hopefully, they continue to check the Web from time to time, part of a monitoring practice that is important in the business of identifying early warning signals that can damage reputations and more.

True, there are services and software that will monitor periodically or continuously. Some are good, while others are next to worthless and actually do damage by engendering a false sense of confidence—and that's always bad.

Cost is a factor, too. The better solutions can be expensive, so many executives dismiss the need or practicality of them. "Besides, it won't happen to me," is a frequent refrain. But executed efficiently and effectively, such solutions can provide early warnings and therefore value through improved risk management.

Sometimes the security organizations will want to conduct this service internally. While that can be cost-efficient, make sure someone is watching the watchers. There have been occasions where insiders have been responsible for the attacks and end up extorting, or planning to extort, the victims. Also, tracking their own histories on the Web may not be an effective use of executive time. Plus, they may not be very good at it. The Web is a giant, often intricate destination, and searching it definitively and regularly is not always satisfying in terms of results.

Recommendation: Try if you want, but best to leave it to the professionals and consider it a cost of doing business in the cyber-intensive twenty-first century. The chances are that these types of attacks, which are really the compromise of intellectual property and brand value, are going to increase, and significantly if not dramatically. The reason is that these crimes are relatively easy to commit, the financial payoff is substantial, and the risk to the criminals is low. This is a bad combination.

As in everyday life, the familiar sometimes—often, actually—becomes, well, familiar. The result is that familiarity breeds acceptance, even trust. Working around others in the same company breeds familiarity, often followed by trust. If someone is hired, many colleagues confer to that person a degree of trust, assuming that there is every reason to trust their colleague and no reason not to. That's when early warning signals are sometimes ignored. Some employees may even feel disloyal or paranoid in experiencing these early warning signals. Trust makes people feel good, and life is tough enough. Work can be challenging. We want to accept and be accepted. But sometimes that's a mistake. And sometimes that early warning signal is not just paranoia.

Other signals are ignored, too. Ever take a walk at night in a strange part of town? Did you feel on edge, perhaps a bit nervous, even uncertain about what could happen? You see people you don't know. Maybe they are following you. You think they may represent a threat. Things race through your mind. Are they really threatening or is just a fertile imagination at work? You shake it off. Nothing to worry about. But then you are attacked—physically assaulted.

Early warning signals exist, in nature and in the workplace. It's important to recognize them and to act on them, in the workplace and elsewhere. In human beings, it is actually a biological and chemical early warning, but one that is often ignored. Ironically, because of the desire to trust, early warning signals are not trusted. These sensations are often ignored. But that doesn't diminish their importance. These are signals that kept early man alive, when receiving such a signal caused fight or flight, simple internal reactions that made a difference.

Early warning signals of every kind have value. Recognizing them, understanding them, and acting upon them is the key. Remember, it's not paranoia if it's really happening. Given the volume, the types, and the severity of information breaches, the evidence suggests this is not about paranoia.

Companies with prior breaches often had early warnings. The signals failed to garner much attention. Some of the signals were simply not observed—invisible signals. Some were observed but ignored. Of course, sometimes there are no early warning signals. The attacks just happen. But not always.

Here's another early warning signal that, surprisingly, many companies miss. It's not a technical signal, nor is it a behavioral one. When vetting external vendors that are going to have access to sensitive data, take a look at the third-party vendor's history. Not only should that company be queried regarding its breach history, but that history should be independently verified. It's possible that employees involved in the negotiation may not be aware of certain breaches, or they may fail to disclose the breaches.

One vendor, unbeknownst to some of its customers, had a breach history stretching over more than a decade. Either the customer companies didn't look or they didn't care. But the failure to identify the prior breach history was a missed early warning signal, one that resulted in a serious data breach. Think about this for a moment. Would you engage a vendor that had a record of more than a decade of serious data breaches? How would that be justified? Would this pass a risk committee of the board? Would it pass a vendor management committee? Maybe it would pass due diligence, based on mitigating actions undertaken by the vendor, cost of services, and a variety of other factors. There may be valid reasons to select that vendor or, in the case of an existing vendor, to continue to use its services. But the real issue would be if the damning information had never been identified. And this is an early warning indicator that would cost virtually nothing. Type the vendor's name into a search engine and see what pops up.

With so much information available today through publicly available information on public- and private-sector web sites, there's really no excuse for not conducting some level of due diligence before selecting a vendor. Still, this does happen. Frequently, that early warning signal is already on the Web, posted on multiple web sites. You've just got to search for it.

Failing to uncover serious breaches, and especially problematic breach histories, never looks good when the board or directors and executive management question what went wrong. "How could this have happened? That company's history of data breaches is all over the Internet!"

These are the words no one wants to hear. But more and more, these words are heard, and the consequences are never pleasant.

Ignoring early warning signals can prove costly. But just like taking that annual physical at the doctor's office, it is far preferable to detect any malady before it can take hold and cause real damage.

There are many challenges ahead; that much is clear. But what is to be done about it? There's ample reason to be optimistic about the cyber future, not because cyber attacks are going to stop, but because the quest to more effectively manage the cyber future will hopefully result in a more trustworthy enterprise and a more robust community of transactional commerce. But a more trustworthy cyber environment will not just happen. It will not result solely from voluntary participation, nor will it result exclusively through regulating what we must protect and how we must protect it. The challenge ahead is uphill, even daunting, but it is not impossible.

Consider the irony that the Internet was devised by optimists in pursuit of avoiding unparalleled disaster. More of that thinking is needed. This is the thinking of an optimist. It is the optimist who examines the threat of a cyber breach and concludes that there is an opportunity to improve the organization's condition, reinforcing its reputation and brand, and thereby designing its future. An optimist will assess the risk and act upon it in confidence, knowing that this is an opportunity to persevere, prepare, and to invest in the values that are so vital to the preservation of trust and the future.

We do not know what the future holds because it isn't here, yet. We get to design it, or at least elements of it, and we do that because we believe there is merit and obligation in doing so. The Brazilian novelist Paulo Coelho wrote that "None of us knows what might happen even the next minute, yet still we go forward. Because we trust. Because we have Faith." Despite the rampant cyber lawlessness and crime that threatens the integrity of seemingly every aspect of commerce and privacy and humanity, we must rise above these threats. Crime will continue, as it has since the beginning of time. Technology will continue to evolve, and companies will continue to adapt to the new ways and means of doing things that are enabled by increasingly complex technology that is supposed to make our lives and our work simpler.

The cyber war is a winnable war, although not one without casualties; the evidence of loss is all around us. Large ships turn slowly, while agile threats move at the speed of light and with near invisibility. We have to turn this massive global vessel rich with the assets resulting from secure commerce and face the cyber threat head-on. We simply have to commit to aggressively addressing the cyber threat and skillfully manage the risks that come with it. Serious choices are demanded of us, and serious consequences will accompany inaction. We must have faith in our resolve and in its result, and we must act now. Mark Twain wrote, "God created war so that Americans would learn geography." Maybe the cyber threat was invented so that we will learn the limits of technology and wake up to its risk.

About the Author

B ORN AND raised in Jacksonville, Florida, **N. MacDonnell Ulsch** is currently a managing director of cyber crime and breach response at a large international consulting firm. He graduated from the University of North Florida and was a lecturer at Boston University. Mr. Ulsch is the author of a previous book, *Threat! Managing Risk in a Hostile World.* He has investigated many high-impact cyber breach and technology espionage cases and advises a diverse range of private-sector and government clients on the cyber threat, how to manage a cyber attack when it occurs, and how to reduce the risk impact of one. He served on the U.S. Secrecy Commission and has appeared on Fox News, ABC News, and other media outlets and has been quoted in many publications, including academic and military studies. The author and his wife, Susan, live near Boston.

Index